The
Imitation
of
Christ

The Imitation of Christ

Thomas a Kempis

Edited by
Paul M. Bechtel

MOODY PRESS
CHICAGO

MOODY PRESS EDITION
1980
Moody Paperback Edition, 1984

8 9 10 11 12 Printing/AK/Year 93 92 91 90 89
Library of Congress
Cataloging in Publication Data

Imitatio Christi.   English.
The imitation of Christ.

I. Thomas a Kempis, 1380—1471.
BV4821.145 1980   242   79—27467
ISBN-8024-4005-3

PUBLISHER'S PREFACE

Although this edition is styled for the modern reader, we have chosen not to make a paraphrase but to retain the spirit of earlier editions. Dr. Paul Bechtel, drawing from his long career in the literary field, has prepared this volume by working chiefly from an edition published in the first half of the nineteenth century by Hurst & Co. and by comparing it with other reliable editions to arrive at the best reading. The Hurst edition, according to its preface (dated 1843), is an English "translation . . . chiefly copied from one printed at London in 1677: but by whom prepared it does not appear. The Latin edition (including the Index) which has been principally followed, is that of Herbert Rosweyd, printed at Antwerp in 1617." Dr. Bechtel has modernized archaisms unfamiliar to the twentieth-century reader, but the basic text remains close to early translations of this devotional classic.

It is our prayer that this edition will encourage a rediscovery of one of the finest treasures of our Christian heritage.

CONTENTS

THE SECOND BOOK

Admonitions Tending to Things Internal

THE THIRD BOOK

Of Internal Consolations

THE FOURTH BOOK

Concerning the Sacrament

A Devout Exhortation to the Holy Communion   page 273

Introduction

The Imitation of Christ has been called the best-loved, most widely read religious book in the world, after the Bible. Though it is now no longer true, it was said early in this century that Thomas a Kempis's little book was on the press somewhere in the world every day in the year, every year. In an increasingly secular age like the present, however, the popularity of *The Imitation of Christ* has waned. But the book is still cherished by many readers who are familiar with the spiritual riches of its pages.

Since the appearance of the first manuscripts of *The Imitation* around 1427, the book has spanned the ages and crossed the continents. By 1450 more than two hundred fifty manuscript copies had been made. Today over seven hundred manuscript copies are known. The first printed edition, made with Gutenberg's new movable type, appeared in 1472. The first French edition was printed in Paris in 1481; the first Italian edition in 1483. The latter was reprinted fifty times before 1500. By the end of the nineteenth century, 600 editions had been printed in Latin, 300 in Italian, 350 in German, and uncounted hundreds of editions of this choicest devotional handbook of the Middle Ages had been made in English.

Thomas a Kempis (so named from his birthplace, the walled city of Kempen near Cologne, Germany) was born in 1379. The family name was Hamerken, meaning "Little Hammer," which suggests that his father was an artisan of metals. His mother conducted a school for small children. When Thomas was about twelve and eager for an education, he set out, at his parents' urging, on an eighty-mile walk to the town of Devanter, Holland, where he hoped to enter the Cathedral school. Here his older brother John had come several years before to join a small order founded by Gerard Groote and then supervised by Florentius Radewijns.

Having arrived at his destination, Thomas went, at the suggestion of his brother, to the home of Radewijns to seek residence there. For the history of the Christian life and the practice of devotion, as well as the course of Western literature, it was really a momentous day. No one could have foreseen how that boy of thirteen was destined to influence and enrich the spiritual lives of multitudes of readers. Without resources, Thomas could not pay for his room and board, but Radewijns, a kindly man, was drawn to the lad and agreed to house him without charge. Radewijns also provided his books and paid his fees. When his first teacher asked Thomas who had paid his tuition and the boy responded, "Radewijns," the instructor replied, "Take it back to your kind master."

Sometime afterward, Radewijns found a place for Thomas in the home of a pious woman, for his home was not large enough to house both the Brethren of the Common Life and school-boys. After several years Thomas came to live again at the Brethren house. Of those days he later wrote: "All I earned I gave to the community; the rest I needed was given by Florentius. Here I learned to read and write the Holy Scriptures and books on moral subjects, but it was chiefly through the sweet conversation of the Brethren that I was inspired yet more strongly to despise the world."

The Brethren of the Common Life was an undemonstrative order in which people lived peaceful lives, obeyed the laws of the land, never reacted to rebellion or public demonstration, and never were inflamatory figures as some of the great reformers were. Their outreach was to preach love, obedience, and humility. They busied themselves with works of goodness and compassion, feeding the hungry, sheltering the homeless, caring for the ill, encouraging public reforms, and promoting reforms within the church and monastic orders, where there were often dissensions. Their commitment to quality education led to the development of Brother-hood schools all over Germany and Holland.

Members of the Brethren of the Common Life worked at regular trades, instead of collecting alms as the religious orders did. Many of them served as copyists or artistic illuminators of manuscripts, placing their earnings in a common fund controlled by the order. Simplicity of life was their social ideal, as they believed it was set forth in the *Acts*. Unlike the monastic orders, which stressed the contemplative life, the Brethren emphasized Christian service in the practical affairs of everyday life.

At the age of twenty, Thomas a Kempis left the Brethren and resolved to enter an Augustinian order at the monastery at Mount Saint Agnes, beyond the walls of Zwölle. Like the others in the monastery, he accepted the threefold vow of poverty, chastity, and obedience. In 1413, at the age of thirty-three, he became a priest. In 1425 he was made a subprior of the order, which obligated him to help train novices. For a time he served as treasurer of the monastery but appears to have had little liking for administrative responsibilities.

For seventy years, until the day of his death in 1471 at the age of ninety-two, Thomas dedicated himself to acts of devotion; copying manuscripts (he is said to have copied the Bible four times); writing letters, hymns, and biographies; counseling others; and best of all, compiling *The Imitation of Christ*. Thomas was of the last generation of hand copyists, and his little book the last Christian classic so prepared.

The earliest and best complete manuscrips of *The Imitation of Christ*, now preserved in Brussels, ends with the words "finished and completed in the year of our Lord 1441 by the hands of Brother Thomas Kempis in Mount Saint Agnes near Zwolle." The statement does not name Thomas as the author, nor does it attribute the work to another. Some scholars have assigned the book to Gerard Groote, founder of the Brethren of the Common Life, and assert that Thomas a Kempis was the editor. Groote wrote much of it, it is said, during the last year of his life, after his license to preach had been withdrawn by the church because he was regarded as unsympathetic to many of the ecclesiastical practices of his time. However, claims for Groote's authorship may well be questioned, for none of the existing early manuscripts carry his name, and none of Groote's contemporaries attributes the manuscript to him. There appears to be no way at this date of resolving the issue, and for most readers the name of Thomas a Kempis seems permanently fixed as the author of *The Imitation of Christ*.

The book has as its foundation biblical texts—more than a thousand of them—a wonderful mosaic of arrangement, brought together in an organic union. Its secret as a devotional classic lies in its constant drawing of refreshing strength from the Scriptures; nearly every book of the Bible is represented, though it draws chiefly from the Psalms, the gospels, and the epistles.

Central to the counsel of *The Imitation* is the

assumption that the true Christian should, as far as possible, attempt to imitate the model given him in the life and work of Christ. To succeed in such an effort means to discover the spiritual, the interior life, and to turn aside from the pursuits of the world. Christlike attitudes— humility, self-discipline, love for others, submission to authority—must be cultivated if a life lived in imitation of Christ is to be realized.

Thomas a Kempis's life of withdrawal from society into a monastic order is clearly evident in *The Imitation*. He made no appeal to history, to men of learning, to intellectual problems, to the events of his own day, in spite of the fact that he was living in tempestuous times when the very foundations of Western civilization appeared to be threatened. At times he seems to have written as a monk to other members of his order. When he speaks of avoiding "personal friendships," for example, he appears to be counseling his brothers of the community against select friendships that would be contrary to the spirit of charity. Friendships within the order he certainly had, but he was careful not to be exclusive.

Thomas's life of retirement from the world may seem to be out of accord with contemporary demands for an active spirituality; yet one of the temptations of modern Christians in our hectic busyness is to forfeit the fruits of contemplation. Often, too, our great heritage of devotional literature, with its invitation to reflective meditation, remains unknown among us. The art of meditation, cherished by earlier generations of believers, is nearly a lost art. With Thomas a Kempis and his little book we may begin a new journey in the life of the spirit to which he invites us.

After having read *The Imitation,* Blaise Pascal wrote: "One expects only a book and finds a man. The deep, pious feeling expressed, the earnestness, the modesty, the unartificial piety of the author, come out in every sentence like the silvery sound of inward genuineness." This book, read in the spirit of consecration, has given guidance to generations of Christian believers of every persuasion throughout the world. Read slowly, reflectively, in brief portions at a time, it can encourage a new commitment to those ultimate values to which Christ calls us. One rejoices in the knowledge that a new edition will add other readers to the company of those who have found springs of living water in Thomas a Kempis's ageless little book.

PAUL M. BECHTEL

Wheaton, Illinois
April 1981

THE FIRST BOOK

Admonitions Useful for a Spiritual Life

CHAPTER 1

*Of the Imitation of Christ, and Contempt of
All the Vanities of the World*

"He that followeth Me, walketh not in darkness,"[1] saith the Lord. These are the words of
Christ, by which we are taught, how we ought
to imitate his life and manners, if we will be
truly enlightened, and be delivered from all
blindness of heart.

Let therefore our chief endeavor be, to
meditate upon the life of Jesus Christ.

2. The doctrine of Christ exceedeth all the
doctrines of holy men; and he that hath the
Spirit, will find therein a hidden manna.

But it falleth out, that many who often hear
the gospel of Christ, are yet but little affected,
because they lack the spirit of Christ.

But whosoever would fully and feelingly
understand the words of Christ, must endeavor
to conform his life wholly to the life of Christ.[1]

---

[1]John 8:12

3. What will it avail thee to dispute profoundly of the Trinity, if thou be lacking in humility, and art thereby displeasing to the Trinity?

Surely high words do not make a man holy and just; but a virtuous life makes him dear to God.

I had rather feel compunction than understand the definition thereof.

If thou didst know the whole Bible by heart, and the sayings of all the philosophers, what would all that profit thee without the love of God,[2] and without grace?

Vanity of vanities, and all is vanity,[3] except to love God, and to serve him only.

This is the highest wisdom, by contempt of the world to tend toward the kingdom of heaven.

4. Vanity therefore it is, to seek after perishing riches, and to trust in them.

It is also vanity to hunt after honors, and to climb to high degree.

It is vanity to follow the desires of the flesh, and to labor for that for which thou must afterward suffer more grievous punishment.

Vanity it is, to wish to live long, and to be careless to live well.

It is vanity to mind only this present life, and not to foresee those things which are to come.

It is vanity to set thy love on that which

---

[2] 1 Cor. 13:2   [3] Eccles. 1:3

speedily passes away, and not to hasten thither where everlasting joy abides.

5. Call often to mind that proverb that, "The eye is not satisfied with seeing, nor the ear filled with hearing."[4]

Endeavor therefore to withdraw thy heart from the love of visible things, and to turn thyself to the invisible.

For they that follow their lusts, do stain their own consciences, and lose the favor of God.

CHAPTER 2

Of Thinking Humbly of Ourselves

All men naturally desire to know;[1] but what does knowledge avail without the fear of God?

Surely an humble husbandman that serveth God is better than a proud philosopher that, neglecting himself, laboreth to understand the course of the heavens.

Whoso knoweth himself well, is lowly in his own sight and delighteth not in the praises of men.

If I understood all things in the world, and were not charitable what would that help me in the sight of God, who will judge me according to my deeds?

---

[4]Eccles. 1:8   [1]Eccles. 1:13

2. Cease from an inordinate desire of knowing, for therein is much distraction and deceit.

The learned are well-pleased to seem so to others, and to be accounted wise.[2]

There are many things, which to know is of little or no profit to the soul:

And he is very unwise, that is intent upon other things than those that may serve for his salvation.

Many words do not satisfy the soul; but a good life comforteth the mind, and a pure conscience giveth great assurance in the sight of God.

3. How much the more thou knowest, and how much the better thou understandest, so much the more severely shalt thou therefore be judged, unless thy life be also more holy.

Be not therefore extolled in thine own mind for any art or science which thou knowest, but rather let the knowledge given thee make thee more humble and cautious.

If thou thinkest that thou understandest and knowest much; know also that there be many things more which thou knowest not.

Do not seem to be overwise, but rather acknowledge thine own ignorance.[3]

Why wilt thou prefer thyself before others, since there be many more learned, and more skillful in the Scripture than thou art?

If thou wilt know or learn anything profita-

---

[2] 1 Cor. 8:1   [3] Rom. 12:16

bly, desire to be unknown, and to be little esteemed by man.

4. The highest and most profitable reading is the true knowledge and consideration of ourselves.

It is great wisdom and perfection to esteem ourselves as nothing, and to think always well and highly of others.

If thou shouldest see another openly sin, or commit some heinous offence, yet oughtest thou not to esteem the better of thyself; for thou knowest not how long thou shalt be able to remain in good estate.

We are all frail,[4] but thou oughtest to hold none more frail than thyself.

CHAPTER 3

Of the Doctrine of Truth

Happy is he whom truth by itself doth teach,[1] not by figures and words that pass away; but as it is in itself.

Our own opinion and our own sense do often deceive us, and they discern but little.

What availeth it to make a great dispute about dark and hidden things;[2] whereas for

---

[4]Gen. 8:21   [1]Psalm 94:12   [2]Eccles. 3:9-11

being ignorant of them we shall not be so much as reproved at the day of judgment?

It is a great folly to neglect the things that are profitable and necessary, and give our minds to that which is curious and hurtful: we have eyes and see not.[3]

2. And what have we to do with *genus* and *species*?

He to whom the Eternal Word speaketh, is delivered from a world of unnecessary conceptions.

From that one Word are all things, and all speak that one; and this is the beginning, which also speaketh unto us.

No man without that Word understandeth or judgeth rightly.

He to whom all things are one, he who reduceth all things to one, and seeth all things in one; may enjoy a quiet mind, and remain peaceable in God.

O God, who art the truth, make me one with thee in everlasting charity.

It is tedious to me often to read and hear many things: in thee is all that I would have and can desire.

Let all doctors hold their peace; let all creatures be silent in thy sight; speak thou alone unto me.

3. The more a man is united within himself, and becometh inwardly simple, so much the

---

[3]Psalm 115:5

more and higher things doth he understand without labor; for that he receiveth intellectual light from above.[4]

A pure, sincere, and stable spirit is not distracted, though it be employed in many works; because it works all to the honor of God, and inwardly being still and quiet, seeks not itself in anything it doth.

Who hinders and troubles thee more than the unmortified affections of thine own heart?

A good and godly man arranges within himself beforehand those things which he is outwardly to act;

Neither do they draw him according to the desires of an evil inclination, but he ordereth them according to the direction of right reason.

Who hath a greater combat than he that laboreth to overcome himself?

This ought to be our endeavor, to conquer ourselves, and daily to wax stronger and to make a further growth in holiness.

4. All perfection in this life hath some imperfection mixed with it; and no knowledge of ours is without some darkness.

An humble knowledge of thyself is a surer way to God than a deep search after learning;

Yet learning is not to be blamed, nor the mere knowledge of anything whatsoever to be disliked, it being good in itself, and ordained by

---

[4]Matt. 11:25; Luke 10:21

God; but a good conscience and a virtuous life is always to be preferred before it.

But because many endeavor rather to get knowledge than to live well; therefore they are often deceived, and reap either none, or very slender profit.

5. Oh, if men bestowed as much labor in the rooting out of vices, and planting of virtues, as they do in moving of questions, neither would there be so much hurt done, nor so great scandal be given in the world, nor so much looseness be practiced in monasteries.

Truly, at the day of judgment we shall not be examined what we have read, but what we have done;[5] not how well we have spoken, but how virtuously we have lived.

Tell me now, where are all those doctors and masters, with whom thou wert well acquainted, while they lived and flourished in learning?

Now others possess their livings and perhaps do scarce ever think of them. In their lifetime they seemed something, but now they are not spoken of.

6. Oh, how quickly doth the glory of the world pass away![6] Oh, that their life had been answerable to their learning! then had their study and reading been to good purpose.

How many perish by reason of vain learning[7] in this world, who take little care of the serving of God:

---

[5]Matt. 25   [6]Eccles. 2:11   [7]Tit. 1:10

And because they rather choose to be great than humble, therefore they become vain in their imaginations.[8]

He is truly great, that is great in charity.

He is truly great that is little in himself, and that maketh no account of any height of honor.[9]

He is truly wise, that accounteth all earthly things as dung, that he may gain Christ.[10]

And he is truly learned, that doeth the will of God, and forsaketh his own will.

CHAPTER 4

Of Wisdom and Forethought in Our Actions

We must not give ear to every saying or suggestion,[1] but ought with caution and patience to ponder things according to the will of God.

But alas! such is our weakness, that we often rather believe and speak evil of others than good.

Those that are perfect men do not easily give credit to everything one tells them; for they know that human frailty is prone to evil,[2] and likely to fail in words.[3]

---

[8]Rom. 1:21   [9]Matt. 18:4; 23:11   [10]Phil. 3:8
[1]1 John 4:1   [2]Gen. 8:21   [3]James 3:2

2. It is great wisdom not to be rash in thy proceedings,[4] nor to stand stiffly in thine own opinions;

As also not to believe everything which thou hearest, nor presently to relate again to others[5] what thou hast heard or dost believe

Consult with him that is wise and conscientious and seek to be instructed by a better than thyself, rather than to follow thine own inventions.[6]

A good life maketh a man wise before God,[7] and giveth him experience in many things.[8]

The more humble a man is in himself, and the more subject unto God; so much the more prudent shall he be in all his affairs, and enjoy greater peace and quiet of heart.

CHAPTER 5

Of the Reading of Holy Scriptures

Truth, not eloquence, is to be sought for in Holy Scripture.

Each part of the Scripture is to be read with the same spirit in which it was written.[1]

We should rather search after our spiritual profit in the Scriptures, than subtilty of speech.

We ought to read plain and devout books as willingly as high sounding and profound ones.

---

[4]Prov. 19:2   [5]Prov. 17:9   [6]Prov. 12:15
[7]Prov. 15:33   [8]Eccles. 1:16   [1]Rom. 15:4

Let not the authority of the writer offend thee, whether he be of great or small learning; but let the love of pure truth draw thee to read.[2]

Search not who spoke this or that, but mark what is spoken.

2. Men pass away, but the truth of the Lord remaineth for ever.[3] God speaks unto us in different ways, without respect of persons.[4]

Our own curiosity often hindereth us in reading of the Scriptures, when as we will examine and discuss that which we should rather pass over without more attention.

If thou desire to reap profit, read with humility, simplicity, and faithfulness; nor ever desire the reputation of learning.

Inquire willingly, and hear with silence the words of holy men; dislike not the parables of the elders, for they are not recounted without cause.[5]

CHAPTER 6

Of Inordinate Affections

Whensoever a man desireth anything inordinately, he becomes restless in himself.

The proud and covetous can never rest. The poor and humble in spirit live together in all peace.

---

[2] 1 Cor. 2:4   [3] Psalm 117:2; Luke 21:33
[4] Rom. 2:11; 10:12; Col. 3:11   [5] Prov. 1:6; Eccles. 12:9

The man that is not yet perfectly dead to himself, is quickly tempted and overcome in small and trifling things.

The weak in spirit, and he that is yet in a manner carnal and delights in the pleasures of the senses, can hardly withdraw himself altogether from earthly desires:

And therefore he is often afflicted, when he withdraws himself from them, and easily falleth into anger, when any opposition is made against him.

2. And if he hath followed therein his inclination, he is presently disquieted with remorse of conscience; because he yielded to his passion, which profiteth him nothing in obtaining the peace he sought for.

True quietness of heart therefore is gotten by resisting our passions, not by obeying them.

There is then no peace in the heart of a carnal man, nor in him that is addicted to outward things, but in the spiritual and devout man.

CHAPTER 7

Of Fleeing from Vain Hope and Pride

He is vain that putteth his trust in man,[1] or creatures.

Be not ashamed to serve others for the love of

---

[1]Jer. 17:5

Jesus Christ; nor to be esteemed poor in this world.

Presume not upon thyself, but place thy hope in God.[2]

Do what lieth in thy power, and God will assist thy good intention.

Trust not in thine own knowledge,[3] nor in the subtilty of any living creature; but rather in the grace of God, who helpeth the humble, and humbleth those that are proud.

2. Glory not in wealth if thou have it, nor in friends, who are powerful; but in God who giveth all things, and above all desireth to give thee himself.

Extol not thyself for the height of thy stature or beauty of thy person, which may be disfigured and destroyed with a little sickness.

Take not pleasure in thy natural gifts, or intelligence, lest thereby thou displease God, to whom belongs all the good whatsoever thou hast by nature.

3. Esteem not thyself better than others,[4] lest perhaps in the sight of God, who knoweth what is in man, thou be accounted worse than they.

Be not proud of well-doing;[5] for the judgment of God is far different from the judgment of men, and that often offendeth him which pleaseth them.

---

[2]Psalm 31:1   [3]Jer. 9:23
[4]Exodus 3:11   [5]Job 9:20

If there be any good in thee, believe that there is much more in others, that so thou mayest preserve humility within thee.

It is not harmful unto thee to debase thyself under all men; but it is very injurious to thee to prefer thyself before any one man.

The humble enjoy continual peace, but in the heart of the proud is envy, and frequent indignation.

CHAPTER 8

That Too Much Familiarity Is to Be Shunned

Lay not thy heart open to every one; but discuss thy affairs with the wise and such as fear God.[1]

Converse not much with young people and strangers.[2]

Flatter not the rich: neither do thou appear willingly before great personages.

Keep company with the humble and plain ones, with the devout and virtuous; and confer with them of those things that may edify. Be not familiar with any woman; but in general commend all good women to God.

Desire to be familiar with God alone and his angels, and avoid the acquaintance of men.

2. We must have charity toward all, but familiarity is not expedient.

---

[1]Eccles. 8:12   [2]Prov. 5:10

Sometimes it happens, that a person unknown to us is much esteemed, from the good report given of him by others; whose presence nevertheless is not pleasing to the eyes of the beholders.

We think sometimes to please others by our company, and we rather offend them with those bad qualities which they discover in us.

CHAPTER 9

Of Obedience and Subjection

It is a great thing to live in obedience, to be under a superior, and not to be our own judges.

It is much safer to obey than to govern.

Many live under obedience, rather for necessity than for love; such are discontented, and do easily suffer. Neither can they attain to freedom of mind, unless they willingly and heartily put themselves under obedience for the love of God.

Go whither thou wilt, thou shalt find no rest, but in humble subjection under the government of a superior. The imagination and change of places have deceived many.

2. True it is, that every one willingly doth that which agreeth with his own tastes; and is apt to esteem those most that are of his own mind;

But if God be among us, we must sometimes cease to adhere to our own opinion for the sake of peace.

Who is so wise that he can fully know all things?

Be not therefore too confident in thine own opinion; but be willing to hear the judgment of others.

If that which thou thinkest is good, and yet thou partest with it for God, and followest the opinion of another, it shall be better for thee.

3. I have often heard, that it is safer to hear and take counsel, than to give it.

It may also happen, that each one's opinion may be good; but to refuse to yield to others when reason, or a special cause requireth it, is a sign of pride and wilfulness.

CHAPTER 10

Of Avoiding Superfluity in Words

Fly the tumult of the world as much as thou canst;[1] for the talk of worldly affairs is a great hinderance, although it be done with sincere intention;

For we are quickly defiled and enthralled with vanity.

---

[1] Matt. 5:1; 14:23; John 6:15

Oftentimes I could wish that I had held my peace, when I have spoken; and that I had not been in the company of men.

Why do we so willingly speak and talk one with another, when we seldom return to silence before we have hurt our conscience?[2]

The cause why we so willingly talk, is that by discoursing one with another, we seek to receive comfort one of another, and desire to ease our mind over-wearied with thoughts:

And we very willingly talk and think of those things which we most love or desire; or of those which we feel most troublesome unto us.

2. But alas, oftentimes in vain, and to no end; for this outward comfort is the cause of no small loss of inward and divine consolation.

Therefore we must watch and pray, lest our time pass away idly.

If it be lawful and expedient for thee to speak, say those things that may edify.

An evil custom and neglect of our own good doth give too much liberty to inconsiderate speech.

Yet devout conversation of spiritual things do greatly further our spiritual growth, especially when persons of one mind and spirit be gathered together in God.[3]

---

[2]Matt. 7:1; Rom. 2:1   [3]Acts 1:14; Rom. 15: 5-6

CHAPTER 11

Of the Obtaining of Peace, and Zealous Desire for Progress in Grace

We might enjoy much peace, if we would not busy ourselves with the words and deeds of other men, with things which do not concern ourselves.

How can he abide long in peace, who thrusts himself into the cares of others, who seeks occasions abroad, who little or seldom concentrates his own thoughts?

Blessed are the single-hearted: for they shall enjoy much peace.

2. What is the reason why some of the saints were so perfect and contemplative?

Because they labored to mortify themselves wholly to all earthly desires; and therefore they could with their whole heart fix themselves upon God, and be free for spiritual contemplation.

We are too much led by our passions, and too solicitous for transitory things.

We also seldom overcome any one vice perfectly, and are not inflamed with a fervent desire to grow better every day; and therefore we remain cold and lukewarm.

3. If we were perfectly dead unto ourselves, and not entangled within our own breasts, then should we be able to taste divine things, and to have some experience of heavenly contemplation.

The greatest, and indeed the whole impediment, is that we are not disentangled from our passions and lusts, neither do we endeavor to enter into that path of perfection which the saints have walked before us; and when any small adversity befalleth us, we are too quickly dejected, and turn ourselves to human comforts.

4. If we would endeavor, like men of courage, to stand in the battle, surely we should feel the favorable assistance of God from heaven.

For he who giveth us occasion to fight, to the end we may get the victory, is ready to succor those that fight manfully, and do trust in his grace.

If we esteem our progress in religious life to consist only in some exterior observances, our devotion will quickly be at an end.

But let us lay the axe to the root, that being freed from passions, we may find rest to our souls.

5. If every year we would root out one vice, we should soon become perfect men.

But now oftentimes we perceive on the contrary that we were better and purer at the beginning of our conversion, than after many years of our profession.

Our fervor and progress should increase daily: but now it is accounted a great matter, if a man can retain but some part of his first zeal.

If we would but a little force ourselves at the

beginning, then should we be able to perform all things afterward with ease and delight.

6. It is a hard matter to leave off that to which we are accustomed, but it is harder to go against our own wills.

But if thou dost not overcome little and easy things, how wilt thou overcome harder things?

Resist thy inclination in the very beginning, and unlearn evil habits, lest perhaps by little and little they draw thee to greater difficulty.

O, if thou didst but consider how much inward peace unto thyself, and joy unto others, the example of thy holy life would bring, I suppose thou wouldest be more careful of thy spiritual progress.

CHAPTER 12

Of the Profit of Adversity

It is good that we have sometimes some troubles and crosses; for they often make a man enter into himself, and consider that he is here in banishment, and ought not to place his trust in any worldly thing.

It is good that we be sometimes contradicted; and that men think ill or inadequately of us, even though we do and intend well.

These things help often to the attaining of humility, and defend us from vain glory: for then we chiefly seek God for our inward witness, when outwardly we are condemned by men, and when there is no credit given unto us.

2. And therefore a man should rest himself so fully in God, that he need not to seek many comforts of men.

When a good man is afflicted, tempted, or troubled with evil thoughts, then he understandeth better the great need he hath of God, without whom he perceiveth he can do nothing that is good.

Then, also, he sorroweth, lamenteth, and prayeth, by reason of the miseries he suffereth.

Then he is weary of living longer, and wisheth that death would come, that he might be dissolved and be with Christ.

Then also he well perceiveth, that perfect security and full peace can not be had in this world.

CHAPTER 13

Of Resisting Temptation

So long as we live in this world we can not be without tribulation and temptation.

According as it is written in Job, "The life of man upon earth is a life of temptation."[1]

Every one therefore ought to be careful about his temptations, and to watch in prayer, lest the

---

[1] Job 7:1, marginal translation, "warfare."

devil find an occasion to deceive him; who never sleepeth, but goeth about seeking whom he may devour.

No man is so perfect and holy, but he hath sometimes temptations; and altogether without them we can not be.

2. Nevertheless, temptations are often very profitable to us, though they be troublesome and grievous; for in them a man is humbled, purified, and instructed.

All saints passed through many tribulations and temptations, and profited thereby.

And they that could not bear temptations, became reprobate, and fell away.

There is no order so holy, nor place so secret, where there be not temptations, or adversities.

3. There is no man that is altogether free from temptations while he liveth on earth: for in ourselves is the root thereof, being born with an inclination to evil.

When one temptation or tribulation goeth away, another cometh; and we shall ever have something to suffer, because we are fallen from the state of our happiness.

Many seek to flee temptations, and fall more grievously into them.

By flight alone we can not overcome, but by patience and true humility we become stronger than all our enemies.

4. He that only avoideth them outwardly, and doth not pluck them up by the roots, shall profit little; yea, temptations will the sooner

return unto him, and he shall feel himself in a worse state than before.

By little and little, and by patience with long-suffering through God's help, thou shalt more easily overcome, than with violence and thine own importunity.

Often take counsels in temptations, and deal not roughly with him that is tempted; but give him comfort, as thou wouldest wish to be done to thyself.

5. The beginning of all evil temptations is inconstancy of mind, and little trust in God.

For as a ship without a helm is tossed to and fro with the waves, so the man who is remiss, and apt to leave his purpose, is in many ways tempted.

Fire trieth iron, and temptation a just man.

We know not oftentimes what we are able to do, but temptations show us what we are.

Yet we must be watchful, especially in the beginning of the temptation; for the enemy is then more easily overcome, if he is not suffered to enter the door of our hearts, but is resisted without the gate at his first knock.

Wherefore someone said, "Withstand the beginnings, for later the remedy comes too late."[2]

For first there cometh to the mind a bare thought, then a strong imagination, afterward, delight, an evil motion, and then consent.

---

[2]Ovid., lib. 1, de Remed Am.

And so by little and little our wicked enemy getteth complete entrance, while he is not resisted in the beginning.

And the longer a man is negligent in resisting, so much the weaker does he become daily in himself, and the enemy stronger against him.

6. Some suffer great temptations in the beginning of their conversion; others at the end.

Others again are much troubled almost through the whole of their life.

Some are easily tempted, according to the wisdom and equity of the Divine appointment, which weigheth the states and worth of men, and ordaineth all things for the welfare of his own chosen ones.

7. We ought not therefore to despair when we are tempted, but so much the more fervently to pray unto God, that he will grant us help in all tribulations; who, surely, according to the words of St. Paul, will give with the temptation a way of escape, that we may be able to bear it.[3]

Let us therefore humble our souls under the hand of God in all temptations and tribulations, for he will save and exalt the humble in spirit.

8. In temptations and afflictions a man is proved how much he hath profited; and his reward is thereby the greater, and his graces do more eminently shine forth.

Neither is it any such great thing if a man be

---

[3]1 Cor. 10:13

devout and fervent, when he feeleth no affliction; but if in time of adversity he bear himself patiently, there is hope then of great progress in grace.

Some are kept from great temptations, and in small ones which do daily occur, are often overcome; to the end that, being humbled, they may never presume on themselves in great matters, who are baffled in so small things.

CHAPTER 14

Of Avoiding Rash Judgment

Turn thine eyes unto thyself, and beware thou judge not the deeds of other men.[1] In judging of others a man laboreth in vain, often errs, and easily sins;[2] but in judging and examining himself, he always laboreth fruitfully.

We often judge things according as we fancy them; for self-love bereaves us easily of true judgment.

If God were always the pure intention of our desire, we should not be so easily troubled, through the resistance of our carnal mind.

2. But oftentimes something lurketh within, or else occurreth from without, which draweth us after it.

---

[1]Matt. 7:1; Rom. 15:1   [2]Matt. 12:25; Luke 12:51

Many secretly seek self-advantage in what they do, and know it not.

They seem also to live in good peace of mind, when things are done according to their will and opinion; but if things happen otherwise than they desire, they are at once moved and much vexed.

The diversities of judgments and opinions cause oftentimes dissensions between friends and countrymen, between religious and devout persons.[3]

3. An old custom is not easily broken,[4] and no man is willing to be led farther than he can see.

If thou dost more rely upon thine own reason or industry, than upon that power which brings thee under the obedience of Jesus Christ, it will be long before thou become enlightened; for God will have us perfectly subject unto him, that being inflamed with his love, we may transcend the narrow limits of human reason.

CHAPTER 15

Of Works Done in Charity

For no worldly thing, nor for the love of any man, is any evil to be done;[1] but yet, for the

---

[3]Eccles. 3:16   [4]Jer. 13:23   [1]Matt. 18:8

welfare of one that standeth in need, a good work is sometimes to be postponed without any scruple, or changed also for a better.

For by doing this, a good work is not lost, but changed into a better.

Without love the exterior work profiteth nothing;[2] but whatsoever is done of love, be it never so little and contemptible in the sight of the world, it becomes wholly fruitful.

For God weigheth more with how much love a man worketh, than how much he doeth. He doeth much that loveth much.

2. He doeth much, that doeth a thing well.

He doeth well that rather serveth the community than his own will.[3]

Oftentimes it seemeth to be love, and it is rather carnality; because natural inclination, self-will, hope of reward, and desire of our own interest, will seldom be absent.

3. He that hath true and perfect love, seeketh for himself nothing;[4] but only desireth in all things that the glory of God should be exalted.

He also envieth none; because he seeks no private good; neither will he rejoice in himself; but wisheth above all things to be made happy in the enjoyment of God.[5]

He attributeth nothing that is good to any man, but wholly referreth it unto God, from

---

[2] 1 Cor. 13:3; Luke 7:47   [3] Phil. 2:17
[4] Phil. 2:21; 1 Cor. 13:5   [5] Psalm 17:15; 24:6

whom as from the fountain all things proceed; in whom finally all the saints do rest as in their highest fruition.

Oh, he that hath but one spark of true love, would certainly discern that all earthly things be full of vanity.

CHAPTER 16

Of Bearing with the Defects of Others

Those things that a man can not amend in himself or in others, he ought to suffer patiently, until God order things otherwise.

Think that perhaps it is better so for thy trial and patience, without which all our good deeds are not much to be esteemed.

Thou oughtest to pray nevertheless, when thou hast such impediments, that God would grant thee help, and that thou mayest bear them kindly.[1]

2. If one that is once or twice warned will not listen, contend not with him: but commit all to God, that his will may be fulfilled,[2] and his name honored in all his servants, who well knoweth how to turn evil into good.

Endeavor to be patient in bearing with the defects and infirmities of others, of what sort

---

[1]Matt. 6:13; Luke 11:4   [2]Matt. 6:10

soever they be; for that thyself also hast many failings which must be borne with by others.[3]

If thou canst not make thyself such a one as thou wouldest, how canst thou expect to have another fashioned to thy liking?

We would willingly have others perfect, and yet we amend not our own faults.

3. We will have others severely corrected, and will not be corrected ourselves.

The large liberty of others displeaseth us; and yet we will not have our own desires denied us.

We will have others kept under by strict laws; but in no way will ourselves be restrained.

And thus it appeareth, how seldom we weigh our neighbor in the same balance with ourselves.

If all men were perfect, what should we have to suffer of our neighbor for God?

4. But now God hath thus ordered it, that we may learn to bear one another's burdens;[4] for no man is without fault; no man but hath his burden; no man sufficient of himself; no man wise enough of himself; but we ought to bear with one another, comfort one another, help, instruct, and admonish one another.[5]

Occasions of adversity best discover how great virtue or strength each one hath.

For occasions do not make a man frail, but they reveal what he is.

[3] 1 Thess. 5:14; Gal. 6:1   [4] Gal. 6:2
[5] 1 Thess. 5:14; 1 Cor. 12:25

CHAPTER 17

Of a Retired Life

Thou must learn to break thy own will in many things, if thou wilt have peace and concord with others.[1]

It is no small matter to dwell in a religious community, or congregation, to converse therein without complaint, and to persevere therein faithfully until death.[2]

Blessed is he that hath there lived well, and ended happily.

If thou wilt persevere in grace as thou oughtest, and grow therein, consider thyself as a banished man, and a pilgrim upon earth.[3]

Thou must be contented for Christ's sake to be considered as a fool in this world, if thou desire to lead a religious life.

2. The wearing of a religious habit, and shaving of the crown, do little profit, but change of manners, and perfect mortification of passions, make a truly religious man.

He that seeketh anything else but God only, and the salvation of his soul, shall find nothing but tribulation and sorrow.[4]

Neither can he remain long in peace, who does not seek to be the least, and subject unto all.

---

[1]Gal. 6:1   [2]Luke 16:10   [3]1 Pet. 2:11
[4]Eccles. 1:17-18; Ecclus. 1:18

3. Thou camest to serve, not to rule.[5] Know that thou wast called to suffer and to labor, not to be idle, or to spend thy time in talk.

Here therefore men are proved as gold in the furnace.

Here no man can stand, unless he humble himself with his whole heart for the love of God.

CHAPTER 18

Of the Examples of the Holy Fathers

Consider the lively examples of the holy fathers, in whom true perfection and religion shone;[1] and thou shalt see how little it is, and almost nothing, which we do now in these days.

Alas! What is our life, if it be compared to them!

The saints and friends of Christ served the Lord in hunger and thirst, in cold and nakedness, in labor and weariness, in watchings and fastings, in prayer and holy meditations, in many persecutions and reproaches.

2. Oh, how many and grievous tribulations suffered the apostles, martyrs, confessors, virgins, and all the rest that endeavored to follow the steps of Christ!

For they hated their lives in this world, that they might keep them unto life eternal.[2]

---

[5]Matt. 22:26   [1]Heb. 11   [2]John 12:25

Oh, how strict and self-renouncing a life led those holy fathers in the wilderness![3] How long and grievous temptations suffered they! How often were they assaulted by the enemy! What frequent and fervent prayers offered they to God! What rigorous abstinences did they use! How great zeal and care had they of their spiritual progress! How strong a combat had they for the overcoming of their lusts! How pure and upright intentions kept they toward God!

In the day they labored and in the night they attended to continual prayer: although when they labored, also, they ceased not from mental prayer.

3. They spent all their time with profit; every hour seemed short for the service of God.

And by reason of the great sweetness they felt in contemplation, they forgot the necessity of bodily refreshments.

They renounced all riches, dignities, honors, friends, and kinsfolk;[4] they desired to have nothing which appertained to the world; they scarcely took things necessary for the sustenance of life; they grieved to serve their bodies even in necessity.

Therefore they were poor in earthly things, but very rich in grace and virtues.

Outwardly they were destitute, but inwardly they were refreshed with grace and divine consolation.

---

[3]Matt. 7:14   [4]Matt. 19:29

4. They were strangers to the world, but close and familiar friends to God.[5]

They seemed to themselves as nothing, and to his present world contemptible; but they were precious and beloved in the eyes of God.

They were grounded in true humility, lived in simple obedience, walked in love and patience: and therefore they profited daily in the spirit, and obtained great grace in God's sight.

They were given for an example to all religious men; and they should more provoke us to strive for spiritual excellence, than the number of lukewarm livers should prevail to make us lax.

5. Oh, how great was the fervor of all religious persons in the beginning of their holy institution!

How great was their devotion to prayer! What ambition to excel others in virtue! How exact discipline then flourished! How great reverence and obedience, under the rule of their superiors, observed they in all things.

Their footsteps yet remaining, do testify that they were indeed holy and perfect men; who fighting so valiantly trod the world under their feet.

Now, he is accounted great, who is not a transgressor, and who can with patience endure that which he hath undertaken.

Oh, the lukewarmness and negligence of our

---

[5]James 4:4

times! that we so quickly decline from the ancient fervor, and are come to that pass, that very sloth and lukewarmness of spirit maketh our own life wearisome unto us.

Would to God the desire to grow in virtues did not wholly sleep in thee, who hast often seen the many examples of devout and religious persons!

CHAPTER 19

Of the Exercises of a Good Religious Person

The life of a good religious person ought to be adorned with all virtues;[1] that he may inwardly be such as outwardly he seemeth to men.

And with reason there ought to be much more within, that is perceived without. For God beholdeth us;[2] whom we are bound most highly to reverence wheresoever we are, and to walk in purity,[3] like angels, in his sight.

Daily ought we to renew our purposes, and to stir up ourselves to greater fervor, as though this were the first day of our conversion; and to say:

"Help me, my God, in this my good purpose, and in thy holy service: and grant that I may

---

[1]Matt. 5:48   [2]Psalm 33:13; Heb. 4:12-13
[3]Psalm 15:2

now this day begin perfectly; for that which I have done hitherto is as nothing."

2. According to our purpose shall be the success of our spiritual progress; and much diligence is necessary to him that will show progress.

And if he that firmly purposeth often faileth, what shall he do that seldom purposeth anything, or with little resolution?

It may fall out that in various ways we forsake our purpose; yet the light omission of spiritual exercises seldom passes without some loss to our souls.

The purpose of just men depends not upon their own wisdom, but upon God's grace; on whom they always rely for whatsoever they take in hand.

For man proposes, but God disposes;[4] neither is the way of man in himself.

3. If an accustomed exercise be sometimes omitted, either for some act of piety, or profit to my brother; it may easily afterward be recovered again.

But if out of a weariness, or out of carelessness, we lightly forsake the same, it is a great offence against God, and will be found to be prejudicial to ourselves. Let us do the best we can, we shall still too easily fail in many things.[5]

Yet must we always have a fixed course and

---

[4]Prov. 16:9   [5]Eccles. 7:20

especially against those failings which do most of all hinder us.

We must diligently search into and set in order both the outward and the inward man, because both of them are of importance to our progress in godliness.

4. If thou canst not continually recollect thyself, yet do it sometimes, at least once a day, namely, in the morning or at night.

In the morning fix thy good purpose; and at night examine thyself what thou hast done, how thou hast behaved thyself in word, deed, and thought;[6] for in these perhaps thou hast oftentimes offended both God and thy neighbor.

Gird up thy loins like a man against the evil assaults of the devil; bridle thy riotous appetite, and thou shalt be the better able to keep under all the unruly desires of the flesh.

Never be entirely idle; but either be reading, or writing, or praying, or meditating, or endeavoring something for the public good.

As for bodily exercises they must be used with discretion, neither are they to be practiced of all men alike.

5. Those exercises which are not common are not to be exposed to public view; for things private are practiced more safely at home.

Nevertheless thou must beware thou neglect not those which are common, being more ready

---

[6]Deut. 4

for what is private. But having fully and faithfully accomplished all which thou art bound and enjoined to do, if thou hast any spare time, turn thee to thyself, as thy devotion shall desire.

All can not use one kind of spiritual exercise, but one is more useful for this person, another for that.

According to the seasonableness of times also, various exercises are fitting: some suit better with us on working-days, other on holydays.

In the time of temptation, we have need of some, and of others in time of peace and quietness.

Some we practice when we are pensive, and others when we rejoice in the Lord.

6. About the time of the chief festivals, good exercises are to be renewed, and the prayers of holy men more fervently to be implored.

From festival to festival, we should make some good resolution, as though we were then to depart out of this world, and to come to the everlasting feast in heaven.

Therefore ought we carefully to prepare ourselves at holy times, and to live more devoutly, and to keep more strictly all things that we are to observe, as though we were shortly at God's hands to receive the reward of our labors.

7. But if it be deferred, let us realize that we are not sufficiently prepared, and unworthy yet

of so great glory which shall be revealed in us[7] in due time; and let us endeavor to prepare ourselves better for our departure.

"Blessed is that servant," saith the evangelist St. Luke, "whom his Lord when he cometh shall find watching: verily I say unto you, he shall make him ruler over all his goods."[8]

CHAPTER 20

Of the Love of Solitude and Silence

Seek a convenient time[1] to retire into thyself, and meditate often upon God's lovingkindnesses.

Meddle not with strange writings; but read such things as may rather yield compunction to thy heart, than occupation to thy head.

If thou wilt withdraw thyself from speaking vainly, and from gadding idly, as also from listening to novelties and rumors, thou shalt find leisure enough and suitable for meditation on good things.

The greatest saints avoided the society of men,[2] when they could conveniently, and did rather choose to serve God, in secret.

2. One said, "as often as I have been among

---

[7]Rom. 7:18   [8]Luke 12:43-44; Matt. 24:46-47
[1]Eccles. 3:1   [2]Heb. 11:38

men I returned home less a man than I was before."[3]

And this we find true, when we talk long together. It is easier not to speak a word at all, than not to speak more words than we should.

It is easier for a man to remain home, than to keep himself well when he is abroad.

He therefore that intends to attain to the more inward and spiritual things of religion, must with Jesus depart from the multitude and press of people.[4]

No man doth safely appear abroad, but he who gladly can abide at home, out of sight.

No man speaks securely, but he that holds his peace willingly.[5]

No man ruleth safely, but he that is willingly ruled.

No man securely doth command, but he that hath learned readily to obey.

3. No man rejoiceth securely, unless he hath within him the testimony of a good conscience.

And yet always the security of the saints was full of the fear of God.

Neither were they the less anxious and humble in themselves, because they shone outwardly with grace and great virtues.

But the security of bad men ariseth from pride and presumption, and in the end it deceiveth them.

Although thou seem to be a good religious

---

[3]Seneca, Ep. 8   [4]Matt. 5:1   [5]Eccles. 3:7

man, or a devout hermit, yet never promise thyself security in this life.

4. Oftentimes those who have been in the greatest esteem and account amongst men, have fallen into the greatest danger, by overmuch self-confidence.

Wherefore to many it is more profitable not to be altogether free from temptations, but to be often assaulted, lest they should be too secure, and so perhaps be puffed up with pride; or else too freely give themselves to wordly comforts.

Oh, how good a conscience should he keep, that would never seek after transitory joy, nor ever entangle himself with the things of this world!

Oh, how great peace and quietness should he possess, that would cut off all vain anxiety, and think only upon divine things, and such as are profitable for his soul, and would place all his confidence in God!

5. No man is worthy of heavenly comfort, unless he has diligently exercised himself in holy compunction.

If thou desirest true contrition of heart, enter into thy secret chamber, and shut out the tumults of the world, as it is written, "In your chambers be ye grieved."[6] In thy chamber thou shalt find what abroad thou shalt too often lose.

The more thou visitest thy chamber, the more thou wilt like it; the less thou comest

---

[6]Psalm 4:4

thereunto, the more thou wilt loath it. If in the beginning of thy conversion thou art content to remain in it, and keep to it well, it will afterward be to thee a dear friend, and a most pleasant comfort.

6. In silence and in stillness a religious soul advances herself, and learneth the mysteries of Holy Scripture.

There she findeth rivers of tears, wherein she may every night[7] wash and cleanse herself; that she may be so much the more familiar with her Creator, by how much the farther off she liveth from all worldly disquiet.

Whoso, therefore, withdraweth himself from his acquaintance and friends, God will draw near unto him with his holy angels.

It is better for a man to live privately, and to take care of himself, than to neglect his soul, though he could work wonders in the world.

It is commendable in a religious person seldom to go abroad, to be unwilling to see or be seen.

7. Why art thou desirous to see that which it is unlawful for thee to have? The world passeth away and the lust thereof.

Our sensual desires draw us to rove abroad; but when the time is past, what carriest thou home with thee but a burdened conscience and distracted heart?

A merry going out bringeth often a mournful

[7] Psalm 6:6

return home; and a joyful evening makes many times a sad morning.[8]

So all the carnal joy enters gently, but in the end it bites and stings to death.

What canst thou see elsewhere, which thou canst not see here?[9] Behold the heaven and the earth and all the elements; for of these are all things created.

8. What canst thou see anywhere that can long continue under the sun?

Thou thinkest perchance to satisfy thyself, but thou canst never attain it.

Shouldst thou see all things present before thine eyes, what were it but a vain sight?[10]

Lift up thine eyes[11] to God in the highest, and pray him to pardon thy sins and negligences.

Leave vain things to the vain; but be thou intent upon those things which God hath commanded thee.

Shut thy door upon thee,[12] and call unto thee Jesus, thy beloved.

Stay with him in thy closet, for thou shalt not find so great peace anywhere else.

If thou hadst not gone abroad and hearkened to idle rumors, thou wouldest the better have preserved a happy peace of mind. But since thou delightest sometimes to hear novelties, it is but fit thou suffer for it some disquietude of heart.

---

[8]Prov. 14:13   [9]Eccles 1:10   [10]Eccles. 3:2
[11]Psalm 121:1   [12]Matt. 6:6

CHAPTER 21

Of Compunction of Heart

If thou wilt make any progress in godliness,
keep thyself in the fear of God,[1] and desire not
too much liberty. Restrain all thy senses under
the severity of discipline, and give not thyself
over to foolish mirth.

Give thyself to compunction of heart, and
thou shalt gain much devotion thereby.

Compunction opens the way to much good,
which dissoluteness is ready quickly to destroy.

It is a wonder that any man can ever perfectly
rejoice in this life, if he duly consider, and
throughly weigh his state of banishment, and
the many perils wherewith his soul is sur-
rounded.

2. Through lightness of heart, and small care
for our failings, we become insensible of the real
sorrows of our souls; and so oftentimes we vainly
laugh, when we have just cause to weep.

There is no true liberty nor right joy but in
the fear of God, accompanied with a good
conscience.

Happy is he who can cast off all distracting
impediments, and bring himself to the one
single purpose of holy compunction.

Happy is he who can abandon all that may
defile his conscience or burden it.

---

[1] Prov. 19:23

Resist manfully; one custom overcometh another.

If thou canst let others alone in their matters, they likewise shall not hinder thee in thine.

3. Busy not thyself in matters which concern others: neither entangle thyself with the affairs of thy superiors.

Still have an eye to thyself first, and be sure more especially to admonish thyself before all thy beloved friends.

If thou hast not the favor of men, be not grieved at it;[2] but take this to heart, that thou dost not behave thyself so warily and circumspectly as it becometh the servant of God, and a devout religious man.

It is better often, and safer, that a man should not have many consolations in this life,[3] especially such as are according to the flesh.

But that we have not divine consolations at all, or do very seldom taste them, the fault is ours, because we seek not after compunction of heart, nor do altogether forsake the vain and outward comforts.

4. Know that thou art unworthy of divine consolation, and that thou hast rather deserved much tribulation.

When a man hath perfect contrition, then is the whole world grievous and bitter unto him.[4]

---

[2]Gal. 1:10   [3]Psalm 76:5
[4]Judges 2:4; 20:26; 2 Kings 13

A good man findeth sufficient cause for mourning and weeping.

For whether he consider his own or his neighbor's estate, he knoweth that none liveth here without tribulation.

And the more completely a man looks into himself, so much the more he sorroweth.

Our sins and wickednesses in which we lie so entangled that we can seldom apply ourselves to heavenly contemplations, do minister unto us matter of just sorrow and inward contrition.

5. Didst thou oftener think of thy death[5] than of thy living long, there is no question but thou wouldst be more zealous to improve.

If also thou didst but consider within thyself the infernal pains in the other world,[6] I believe thou wouldst willingly undergo any labor or sorrow in this world, and not be afraid of the greatest austerity.

But because these things enter not to the heart, and we still love those things only that delight us, therefore we remain cold and very dull in religion.

6. It is often our lack of spirit which maketh our miserable bodies so easily complain.

Pray therefore unto the Lord with all humility, that he will grant thee the spirit of compunction. And say with the prophet, "Feed me, O Lord, with the bread of tears, and give me plenteousness of tears to drink."[7]

---

[5]Eccles. 7:1-2   [6]Matt. 25:41   [7]Psalm 80:5

CHAPTER 22

Of the Consideration of Human Misery

Miserable thou art, wheresoever thou be, or wherever thou turnest, unless thou turn thyself unto God.

Why art thou troubled when things succeed not as thou wouldest or desirest? For who is he that hath all things according to his desire?[1] neither I nor thou, nor any man upon earth.

There is none in this world, even though he be king or bishop, without some tribulation or perplexity.

Who is then in the best circumstance? even he who is able to suffer something for God.

2. Many weak and infirm persons say, Behold! what a happy life such an one leads;[2] how wealthy, how great he is, in what power and dignity!

But lift up thine eyes to the riches of Heaven, and thou shalt see that all the goods of this life are nothing. They are very uncertain, and rather burdensome than otherwise, because they are never possessed without anxiety and fear.

Man's happiness consisteth not in having abundance of temporal goods,[3] but a moderate portion is sufficient for him.

---

[1]Eccles. 6:2   [2]Luke 12:19   [3]Prov. 19:1

Truly it is misery even to live upon the earth.[4]

The more spiritual a man desires to be, the more bitter does his present life become to him; because he sees more clearly and perceives more sensibly the defects of human corruption.

For to eat and to drink, to sleep and to watch, to labor and to rest, and to be subject to other necessities of nature, is doubtless a great misery and affliction to a religious man, who would gladly be set loose, and free from all sin.

3. For the inward man is much weighed down with these corporal necessities while we live in this world.

Therefore the prophet prayeth with great devotion to be enabled to be free from them, saying, "Bring me, O Lord, out of my necessities."[5]

But woe be to them that know not their own misery; and a greater woe to them that love this miserable and corruptible life![6]

For some there are who so much doat upon it, that although by labor or by begging they can scarce get mere necessaries, yet if they might be able to live here always, they would care nothing at all for the kingdom of God.

4. Oh, how senseless are these men, and unbelieving in heart, who lie so deeply sunk in

---

[4]Job 14:1; Eccles. 1:17
[5]Psalm 25:17   [6]Rom. 8:22

the earth, that they can relish nothing but carnal things![7]

But miserable as they are, they shall in the end feel to their cost how vile and how worthless that was which they loved.

Whereas the saints of God and all the devout friends of Christ regarded not those things which pleased the flesh, nor those which flourished in this life, but longed after the everlasting riches[8] with their whole hope and earnest intention.

Their whole desire was carried upward to things everlasting and invisible, that the desire of things visible might not draw them to things below.

5. Oh, my brother, lose not thy confidence of making progress in godliness; there is yet time, the hour is not yet passed.[9]

Why wilt thou defer thy good purpose from day to day? Arise and begin in this very instant, and say, "Now is the time to be doing, now is the time to be striving, now is the proper time to amend myself."

When thou art ill at ease and much troubled, then is the time of blessing.

Thou must pass through fire and water[10] before thou come to the place of refreshing.

Unless thou dost earnestly force thyself, thou shalt never get the victory over sin.

---

[7]Rom. 8:5   [8]1 Pet. 1:4; Heb. 11:26
[9]Rom. 13:11; Heb. 10:35   [10]Psalm 46:12

So long as we carry about us this frail body of ours, we can never be without sin, or live without weariness and pain.

We would gladly be quiet and freed from all misery, but because through sin we have lost our innocence, we have together with that lost also the true happiness.[11]

Therefore it becomes us to have patience, and to wait for the mercy of God, till this iniquity pass away, and mortality be swallowed up of life![12]

6. Oh, how great is human frailty, which is always prone to evil![13]

Today thou confessest thy sins, and tomorrow thou committest the very same thou hast confessed.

Now, thou art resolved to look well unto thy ways, and within a while thou so behavest thyself, as though thou hadst never any such purpose at all.

Good cause have we therefore to humble ourselves,[14] and never to have any great conceit of ourselves: since we are so frail and so inconstant.

Besides that may quickly be lost by our own negligence, which, by the grace of God, with much labor we have scarce at length obtained.

7. What will become of us in the end, who begin so early to grow lukewarm!

---

[11] Rom. 7:24; Gen. 3:17   [12] 2 Cor. 5:4
[13] Gen. 6:5; 8:21   [14] 2 Maccab. 9:11

Woe be unto us, if we will so soon give ourselves unto ease, as if all were in peace and safety, when as yet there appears to be no sign of true holiness in our conversation!

We have much need like young beginners to be newly instructed again to good life, if haply there be some hope of future amendment, and greater progress in things spiritual.

CHAPTER 23

Of Meditation on Death

Very quickly there will be an end of thee here;[1] look what will become of thee in another world.

Today the man is here; tomorrow he hath disappeared.

And when he is out of sight, quickly also is he out of mind.

Oh, the stupidity and hardness of man's heart, which thinketh only upon the present, and doth not rather care for what is to come!

Thou oughtest so to order thyself in all thy thoughts and actions, as if today thou wert about to die.[2]

If thou hadst a good conscience, thou wouldst not greatly fear death.[3]

It is better to avoid sins than to flee death.[4]

---

[1]Job 9:25-26; 14:1-2; Luke 12:20; Heb. 9:27
[2]Matt. 25:13   [3]Luke 12:37   [4]Wisd. 4:16

If today thou art not prepared, how wilt thou be so tomorrow?[5]

Tomorrow is uncertain, and how knowest thou that thou shalt live till tomorrow?

2. What availeth it to live long, when there is so small amendment in our practice!

Alas! length of days doth more often make our sins the greater, than our lives the better!

Oh, that we had spent but one day in this world thoroughly well!

Many there are who count how long it is since their conversion; and yet full slender oftentimes is the fruit of amendment in their lives.

If to die be accounted dreadful, to live long may perhaps prove more dangerous.

Happy is he that always hath the hour of his death before his eyes,[6] and daily prepareth himself to die.

If at any time thou hast seen another man die, make account thou must also pass the same way.[7]

3. When it is morning, think thou mayest die before night;

And when evening comes, dare not to promise thyself the next morning.

Be thou therefore always in a readiness, and so lead thy life that death may never take thee unprepared.[8]

Many die suddenly and when they look not

[5]Matt. 24:44; 25:10   [6]Eccles. 7:1
[7]Heb. 9:27   [8]Luke 21:36

for it; for the Son of Man will come at an hour when we think not.[9]

When that last hour shall come, thou wilt begin to have a far different opinion of thy whole life that is past, and be exceeding sorry thou hast been so careless and remiss.

4. Oh, how wise and happy is he that now laboreth to be such a one in his life, as he wisheth to be found at the hour of his death!

A perfect contempt of the world,[10] a fervent desire to excel in virtue, the love of discipline, the painfulness of repentance, the readiness to obey, the denial of ourselves, and the bearing any affliction for the love of Christ, patiently, will give us great confidence we shall die happily.

While thou art in health thou mayest do much good; but when thou art sick, I see not what thou art able to do.

Few by sickness grow better and more reformed; as also they who wander much abroad, seldom thereby become holy.

5. Trust not to friends and kindred, neither do thou put off the care of thy soul's welfare till hereafter; for men will sooner forget thee than thou art aware of.

It is better to look to it betime, and do some good beforehand, than to trust to other men's help.[11]

---

[9]Matt. 24:44; Luke 12:40   [10]Ecclus. 12:1
[11]Isaiah 30:5; 31:1; Jer. 17:5; 48:7; Matt. 6:20

If thou art not careful for thyself now, who will be careful for thee hereafter?

The time that is now present is very precious; now are the days of salvation; now is the acceptable time.

But alas! that thou shouldest spend thy time so idly here, when thou mightest seek to live eternally hereafter.

The time will come, when thou shalt desire one day or hour to amend in, and I can not say that it will be granted thee.

6. O beloved, from how great danger mightest thou deliver thyself, from how great fear free thyself, if thou wouldst be ever fearful and mindful of death!

Labor now to live so, that at the hour of death thou mayest rather rejoice than fear.

Learn now to die to the world, that thou mayest then begin to live with Christ.[12]

Learn now to despise all earthly things,[13] that thou mayest freely live with Christ.

Chastise thy body now by repentance,[14] that thou mayest then have assured confidence.

7. Ah, foolish me, why dost thou think to live long, when thou canst not promise to thyself one day?[15]

How many have been deceived and suddenly snatched away!

How often dost thou hear these reports: Such

---

[12]Rom. 6:8 [13]Luke 14:33
[14]1 Cor. 9:27 [15]Luke 12:20

a man is slain, another man is drowned, a third breaks his neck with a fall from some high place, this man died eating, and that man playing!

One perished by fire, another by the sword, another of the plague, another was slain by thieves. Thus death is the end of all, and man's life suddenly passeth away like a shadow.[16]

8. Who shall remember thee when thou art dead? and who shall pray for thee?

Do, do now, my beloved, whatsoever thou art able to do; for thou knowest not when thou shalt die, nor yet what shall befall thee after thy death.

Now whilst thou hast time, heap unto thyself everlasting riches.[17]

Think on nothing but the salvation of thy soul, care for nothing but the things of God.

Make now friends to thyself by honoring the saints of God, and imitating their actions, that when thou failest in this short life, they may receive thee into everlasting habitations.[18]

Keep thyself as a stranger and pilgrim upon the earth.[19] and as one to whom the affairs of this world do not appertain.

Keep thy heart free, and lifted up to God, because thou hast here no abiding city.[20]

Send heavenward thy daily prayers and sighs,

---

[16]Job 14:2   [17]Matt. 6:20; Luke 12:33; Gal. 6:8
[18]Luke 16:9; Heb. 11   [19]1 Pet. 2:11
[20]Heb. 13:14

together with thy tears, that after death thy spirit may be found worthy with much happiness to pass to the Lord. *Amen.*

CHAPTER 24

Of Judgment, and the Punishment of Sinners

In all things have a special aim to thy end, and how thou wilt be able to stand before that severe Judge[1] to whom nothing is hid, who is not pacified with gifts, nor accepteth any excuses, but will judge according to right and equity.

O wretched and foolish sinner, who sometimes fearest the countenance of an angry man, what answer wilt thou make to God, who knoweth all thy wickedness![2]

Why dost thou not provide for thyself,[3] against that great day of judgment, when no man can excuse or answer for another, but every one shall have enough to answer for himself!

Now are thy pains profitable, thy tears acceptable,[4] thy groans audible, thy grief pacifieth God, and purgeth thy soul.

2. The patient man hath a great and wholesome purgatory,[5] who though he receive inju-

---

[1]Heb. 10:31   [2]Job 9:2   [3]Luke 16:9
[4]2 Cor. 6:4   [5]James 1:4

ries, yet grieveth more for the malice of another than for his own wrong; who prayeth willingly for his adversaries,[6] and from his heart forgiveth their offences; he delayeth not to ask forgiveness of whomsoever he hath offended; he is sooner moved to compassion than to anger; he often offereth a holy violence to himself, and laboreth to bring the body wholly into subjection to the spirit.

It is better to purge out our sins, and cut off our vices here, than to keep them to be punished hereafter.

Verily we do but deceive ourselves through an inordinate love of the flesh.

3. What is that, that infernal fire shall feed upon, but thy sins?

The more thou sparest thyself now and followest the flesh, so much the more hereafter shall be thy punishment, and thou storest up greater fuel for that flame.

In what thing a man hath sinned, in the same shall he be the more severely punished.

There shall the slothful be pricked forward with burning goads, and the gluttons be tormented with hunger and thirst.

There shall the luxurious and lovers of pleasures be bathed in burning pitch and stinking brimstone, and the envious, like mad dogs, shall howl for very grief.

---

[6]Luke 23:34; Acts 7:60

4. There is no sin but shall have its proper punishment.

There the proud shall be filled with all confusion; the covetous shall be pinched with miserable poverty.

One hour of pain there shall be more bitter than a thousand years of the sharpest penitence here!

There is no quiet, no comfort for the damned there:[7] yet here we have some intermission of our labors, and enjoy the comfort of our friends.

Be now solicitous and sorrowful because of thy sins, that at the day of judgment thou mayest be secure with the company of the blessed.

For then shall the righteous with great boldness stand against such as have vexed and oppressed them.[8]

Then shall he stand to judge them, who doth now humbly submit himself to the judgments of men.

Then shall the poor and humble have great confidence, but the proud man shall be seized with fear on every side.

5. Then will it appear that he was wise in this world, who had learned for Christ to be a fool and despised.

Then shall every affliction patiently undergone delight us, when the mouth of iniquity shall be silenced.[9]

---

[7] Job 40:12; 41   [8] Wisd. 5:1   [9] Psalm 107:42

Then shall the devout rejoice, and the profane shall mourn.

Then shall he more rejoice that hath subdued his own flesh, than he that hath abounded in all pleasure and delight.[10]

Then shall the poor attire shine gloriously, and the precious robes seem vile and contemptible.

Then shall be more commended the poor cottage, than the gilded palace.

Then will constant patience satisfy us, more than all earthly power.

Then simple obedience shall be exalted above all worldly wisdom.[11]

6. Then shall a good and clear conscience more rejoice a man, than the profound learning of philosophy.

Then shall the contempt of riches weigh more than all the worldling's treasure.

Then wilt thou be more comforted that thou hast prayed devoutly, than that thou hast fared bountifully.

Then wilt thou be happy that thou hast kept silence, than that thou hast talked much.

Then will good works avail more than many eloquent words.

Then a strict life and severe repentance will be more pleasing than all earthly delights.

Accustom thyself now to suffer a little, that

---

[10]2 Cor. 4:17   [11]Isaiah 29:19

thou mayest then be delivered from more grievous pains.

Prove first here what thou canst endure hereafter.

If now thou canst endure so little, how wilt thou then be able to endure eternal torments?

If now a little suffering make thee so impatient, what will hell-fire do hereafter?

Assure thyself thou canst not have two paradises; it is impossible to enjoy delights in this world, and after that to reign with Christ.

7. Suppose thou hast hitherto lived always in honors and delights, what would all this avail thee if thou wert to die at this instant?[12]

All therefore is vanity,[13] but to love God and serve him only.

For he that loveth God with all his heart, is neither afraid of death nor punishment, nor of judgment, nor of hell; for perfect love gives secure access to God.[14]

But he that takes delight in sin, what wonder is it if he is afraid, both of death and judgment?

Yet it is good, although love cannot withhold thee from sin, that at least the fear of hell should restrain thee.

But he that layeth aside the fear of God, can never continue long in good estate, but falleth quickly into the snares of the devil.

---

[12]Luke 12:20   [13]Eccles. 1:2   [14]Rom. 8:39

CHAPTER 25

Of the Zealous Amendment of Our Whole Life

Be watchful and diligent in the service of God;[1] and often think why thou camest hither, and why thou hast left the world. Was it not that thou mightest live unto God, and become a spiritual man?

Be fervent then in going forward,[2] for shortly thou shalt receive a reward for thy labors; there shall not be then any fear or sorrow within thy sphere.[3]

Labor but now a little, and thou shalt find great rest, yea, perpetual joy.[4]

If thou continuest faithful and zealous in doing good, no doubt but God will be faithful and liberal in rewarding thee.[5]

Thou oughtest to have a good hope[6] for obtaining victory; but thou must not be secure, lest thou grow either negligent or proud.

2. When one man that was in anxiety of mind, often wavering between fear and hope, did once, being oppressed with grief, humbly prostrate himself in a church before the altar in prayer, and said within himself, "Oh, if I knew that I should yet persevere!" he presently heard within him an answer from God, which said,

---

[1]2 Tim. 4:5   [2]Matt. 5:48
[3]Rev. 21:4; 22:3   [4]Ecclus. 51:27; Rev. 21:4; 22:3
[5]Matt. 25:23   [6]Rom. 5:5

"What if thou didst know it, what wouldest thou do? Do now what thou wouldest do then, and thou shalt be secure."

And being herewith comforted and strengthened, he committed himself wholly to the will of God, and that troubling anxiety ceased:

Neither had he any mind to search curiously any further, to know what should befall him; but rather labored to understand what was the perfect and acceptable will of God,[7] for the beginning and accomplishing of every good work.

3. "Hope in the Lord and do good," saith the prophet, "and inhabit the land, and thou shalt be fed with its riches."[8]

One thing there is that draweth many back from a spiritual progress, and the diligent amendment of their lives; namely extreme fear of the difficulty, or the labor of the combat.

However, they above others improve most in virtue, who endeavor most to overcome those things which are most grievous and contrary unto them.

For there a man improveth more and obtaineth greater grace, where he most overcometh himself and mortifieth himself in spirit.

4. But all men have not equally much to overcome and mortify.

Yet he that is diligent, though he have more passions, shall profit more in virtue, than

---

[7] Rom. 12:2   [8] Psalm 37:3

another that is of a more temperate disposition, if he is less fervent in the pursuit of virtue.

Two things especially much further our amendment, namely, to withdraw ourselves violently from that to which nature is viciously inclined, and to labor earnestly for that virtue which we most want.

Be careful also to avoid with great diligence those things in thyself, which do commonly displease thee in others.

5. Gather some profit to thy soul wheresoever thou art; so as if thou seest or hearest of any good examples, stir up thyself to the imitation thereof.

But if thou seest anything worthy of reproof, beware thou do not the same. And if at any time thou hast done it, labor quickly to amend it.

As thine eye observeth others,[9] so art thou also noticed by others.

Oh, how sweet and pleasant a thing it is, to see brethren fervent and devout, well-mannered and well disciplined![10]

And on the contrary, how sad and grievous a thing it is, to see them live in a dissolute and disordered state, not applying themselves to that for which they are called!

How hurtful a thing is it, when they neglect the good purposes of their vocation, and busy

---

[9]Matt. 7:3
[10]Eph. 5 [perhaps 4:1, 16]; 1 Cor. 12:18; Eccles. 3:1

themselves in that which is not committed to their care!

6. Be mindful of the profession thou hast made, and have always before the eyes of thy soul the remembrance of thy Savior crucified.

Thou hast good cause to be ashamed in looking upon the life of Jesus Christ, seeing thou hast not as yet endeavored to conform thyself more unto him, though thou hast been a long time in the way of God.

A religious person that exerciseth himself seriously and devoutly in the most holy life and passion of our Lord, shall there abundantly find whatsoever is necessary and profitable for him; neither shall he need to seek any better thing, than Jesus.

Oh, if Jesus crucified would come into our hearts,[11] how quickly and fully should we be instructed in all truth.

7. A fervent religious person taketh and beareth all well that is commanded him.

But he that is negligent and cold, hath tribulation upon tribulation, and on all sides is afflicted; for he is without inward consolation, and is forbidden to seek external comforts.

A religious person that liveth not according to discipline, lies open to great mischief to the ruin of his soul.

He that seeketh liberty and ease, shall ever

---

[11]Gal. 2:20; 5:14

live in distress, for one thing or another will displease him.

8. Oh, that we had nothing else to do, but always with our mouth, and whole heart to praise our Lord God!

Oh, that thou mightest never have need to eat, nor drink, nor sleep; but mightest always praise God, and only employ thyself in spiritual exercises; thou shouldest then be much happier than now thou art, when for so many necessities thou art constrained to serve the flesh.

Would God these necessities were not at all, but only the spiritual reflections of the soul, which, alas, we taste of too seldom!

9. When a man cometh to that estate, that he seeketh not his comfort from any creature, then doth he begin perfectly to relish God. Then shall he be contented with whatsoever doth befall him in this world.

Then shall he neither rejoice in great matters, nor be sorrowful for small; but entirely and confidently commit himself to God, who shall be unto him all in all;[12] to whom nothing doth perish or die, but all things do live unto him, and serve him in all things without delay.

10. Remember always thy end,[13] and how that time lost never returns. Without care and diligence thou shalt never grow in virtue.

---

²Rom. 11:36; 1 Cor. 8:6; 12:6; 15:28
³Ecclus. 7:36   ¹⁴Rev. 3:16

If thou beginnest to grow cold,[14] it will begin to be evil with thee.

But if thou give thyself to fervor of spirit, thou shalt find much peace, and feel less labor, through the assistance of God's grace, and the love of virtue.

The fervent and diligent man is prepared for all things.

It is harder to resist vices and passions, than to toil in bodily labors.

He that avoideth not small faults, by little and little falleth into greater.[15]

Thou wilt always rejoice in the evening, if thou spend the day profitably.

Be watchful over thyself, stir up thyself, warn thyself, and whatsoever becomes of others, neglect not thyself.

The more holy violence thou usest against thyself, the more shall be thy spiritual advances. Amen.

---

[15]Ecclus. 19:1

THE SECOND BOOK

Admonitions Tending to Things Internal

CHAPTER 1

Of the Inward Life

"The kingdom of God is within you,"[1] saith the Lord. Turn thee with thy whole heart[2] unto the Lord, and forsake this wretched world, and thy soul shall find rest.

Learn to despise outward things, and to give thyself to things inward, and thou shalt see the kingdom of God within thee.

"For the kingdom of God is peace and joy in the Holy Spirit,"[3] which is not given to the unholy.

Christ will come unto thee, and show thee his consolations if thou prepare for him a worthy mansion within thee.

All his glory and beauty is from within,[4] and there is his delight.

---

[1]Luke 17:21   [2]Joel 2:12
[3]Rom. 14:17   [4]Psalm 45:13

The inward man he often visiteth; and hath with him sweet discourses, pleasant solace, much peace, familiarity exceedingly wonderful.

2. O faithful soul, make ready thy heart for this Bridegroom, that he may promise to come unto thee, and dwell within thee.

For thus saith he, "If any love me, he will keep my words, and we will come unto him, and will make our abode with him."[5]

Give therefore admittance unto Christ, and deny entrance to all others.

When thou hast Christ, thou art rich, and hast enough. He will be thy faithful and provident helper in all things, so as thou shalt not need to trust in men.

For men soon change, and quickly fail; but Christ remaineth for ever,[6] and standeth by us firmly unto the end.

3. There is no great trust to be put in a frail and mortal man,[7] even though he be profitable and dear unto us; neither ought we to be much grieved, if sometimes he cross and contradict us.

They that to-day take thy part, tomorrow may be against thee; and often do they turn right around like the wind.

Put all thy trust in God,[8] let him be thy fear,

---

[5]John 14:25   [6]John 12:34   [7]Jer. 17:5
[8]1 Pet. 5:7   [9]Heb. 13:14

and thy love: he shall answer for thee, and will do what is best for thee.

Thou hast not here an abiding city;[9] and wherever thou art, thou art a stranger and pilgrim: neither shalt thou ever have rest, unless thou be most inwardly united with Christ.

4. Why dost thou here gaze about, since this is not the place of thy rest? In heaven ought to be thy home,[10] and all earthly things are to be looked upon as if it were a passing thing.

All things pass away,[11] and thou together with them.

Beware thou cleave not unto them, lest thou be caught, and so perish. Let thy thought be on the Highest, and thy prayer for mercy directed unto Christ without ceasing.

If thou canst not contemplate high and heavenly things, rest thyself in the passion of Christ, and dwell willingly in his sacred wounds.

For if thou flee devoutly unto the wounds and precious marks of the Lord Jesus, thou shalt feel great comfort in tribulation; neither wilt thou much care for the slights of men, and wilt easily bear words of detraction.

5. Christ was also in the world, despised of men, and in greatest necessity, forsaken by his acquaintance and friends, in the midst of slanders.[12]

---

[10]Phil. 3:20   [11]Wisd. 5:9
[12]Matt. 1; 12:24; 16:21; John 15:20

Christ was willing to suffer and be despised; and darest thou complain of any man?

Christ had adversaries and backbiters; and dost thou wish to have all men thy friends and benefactors?

Whence shall thy patience attain her crown,[13] if no adversity befall thee?

If thou art willing to suffer no adversity, how wilt thou be the friend of Christ?

Suffer with Christ, and for Christ, if thou desire to reign with Christ.

6. If thou hadst but once perfectly entered into the inner life of the Lord Jesus, and tasted a little of his ardent love; then wouldst thou not regard thine own convenience, or inconvenience, but rather wouldst rejoice at slanders, if they should be cast upon thee: for the love of Jesus maketh a man despise himself.

A lover of Jesus and of the truth, and a true inward Christian, and one free from inordinate affections, can freely turn himself unto God, and lift himself above himself in spirit, and with joy remain at rest.

7. He that judgeth of all things as they are, and not as they are said or esteemed to be, is truly wise, and taught rather of God than men.[14]

He that can live inwardly, and make small value of outward things, neither requireth

---

[13]2 Tim 2:5   [14]Isaiah 54:13

places, nor expecteth times, for performing of religious exercises.

A spiritual man quickly recollecteth himself, because he never poureth out himself wholly to outward things.

He is not hindered by labor, or business which may be necessary for the time; but as things turn out, so he accommodates himself to them.

He that is well ordered and disposed within himself, cares not for the strange and perverse behavior of men.

A man is hindered and distracted in proportion as he draweth external matters unto himself.

8. If it were well with thee, and thou wert well purified from sin, all things would work out to thee for good,[15] and to thy advancement.

But many things displease, and often trouble thee; because thou art not yet perfectly dead unto thyself, nor separated from all earthly things.

Nothing so defileth and entangleth the heart of man, as the impure love for creatures.

If thou refuse outward comfort, thou wilt be able to contemplate the things of heaven, and often receive inward joy.

---

[15]Rom. 8:28

CHAPTER 2

Of Humble Submission

Think not much who is for thee, or against thee;[1] but mind what thou art about, and take care that God may be with thee in everything thou doest.

Have a good conscience, and God will well defend thee.[2]

For whom God will help, no man's perverseness shall be able to injure.

If thou canst be silent and suffer, without doubt thou shalt see that the Lord will help thee.

He knoweth the time and manner of delivering thee, and therefore thou oughtest to resign thyself unto him.

It is God's purpose to help, and to deliver from all confusion.

It is often very profitable, to keep us more humble, that others know and rebuke our faults.

2. When a man humbleth himself for his failings, then he easily pacifieth others, and quickly satisfieth those that are angry with him.

God protecteth the humble and delivereth him;[3] the humble he loveth and comforteth; unto the humble man he inclineth himself; unto

---

[1] Rom. 8:31; 1 Cor. 4:3   [2] Psalm 28:7
[3] James 3 [perhaps 4:6]; Job 5:11

the humble he giveth great grace; and after his humiliation he raiseth him to glory.

Unto the humble he revealeth his secrets,[4] and sweetly draweth and inviteth him unto himself.

The humble person, when he is rebuked, is yet in sufficient peace; because he resteth on God, and not on the world.

Do not think that thou hast made any progress, unless thou feel thyself inferior to all.

CHAPTER 3

Of a Good Peaceable Man

First, keep thyself in peace, and then shalt thou be able to bring peace to others.

A peaceable man doth more good than he that is learned.

A passionate man turneth even good into evil, and easily believeth evil.

A good peaceable man turneth all things to good.

He that is well in peace, is not suspicious of any man. But he that is discontented and troubled, is tossed with divers suspicions: he is

---

[4]Matt. 11:25   [1]1 Cor. 13:5

neither at rest himself nor suffereth others to be at rest.

He often speaketh that which he ought not to speak; and omitteth that which were best for him to do.

He considereth what others are bound to do,[2] and neglecteth that which he is bound to himself.

First, therefore, have a careful zeal over thyself,[3] and then thou mayest justly show thyself zealous also for thy neighbor's good.

2. Thou knowest well how to excuse and color thine own deeds, but thou art not willing to receive the excuses of others.

It were more just that thou shouldest accuse thyself, and excuse thy brother.

If thou wilt be endured, learn to endure others.[4]

Behold, how far off thou art yet from true charity and humility; for that knows not how to be angry with any, or to be moved with indignation, but only against one's self.

It is no great matter to associate with the good and gentle; for this is naturally pleasing to all, and every one willingly enjoyeth peace, and loveth those best that agree with him.

But to be able to live peaceably with hard and

---

[2]Matt. 7:3   [3]Acts 1 [perhaps 22:3]
[4]Gal. 6:2; 1 Cor. 13:7

perverse persons, or with the disorderly, or such as go contrary to us, is a great grace, and a most commendable and manly thing.

3. Some there are that keep themselves in peace and are in peace also with others.

And there are some that neither are in peace themselves, nor suffer others to be in peace: they are troublesome to others, but always more troublesome to themselves.

And others there are that keep themselves in peace, and study to bring others unto peace.

Nevertheless, our whole peace in this miserable life consisteth rather in humble sufferance, than in not experiencing adversities.

He that can best tell how to suffer, will best keep himself in peace. That man is conqueror of himself, and lord of the world, the friend of Christ, and heir of heaven.

CHAPTER 4

Of a Pure Mind, and Simple Intention

By two wings, a man is lifted up from things earthly, namely, by simplicity and purity.

Simplicity ought to be in our intention; purity, in our affection. Simplicity reaches toward God; purity doth apprehend and taste him.

No good action will hinder thee, if thou be inwardly free from inordinate affection.

If thou intend and seek nothing else but the will of God and the good of thy neighbor, thou shalt thoroughly enjoy internal liberty.

If thy heart were sincere and upright, then every creature would be to thee a mirror of life, and a book of holy doctrine.

There is no creature so small and abject that it representeth not the goodness of God.[1]

2. If thou wert inwardly good and pure,[2] then wouldest thou be able to see and understand all things well without impediment.

A pure heart penetrateth heaven and hell.

Such as every one is inwardly, so he judgeth outwardly.

If there be joy in the world, surely a man of a pure heart possesseth it.

And if there be anywhere tribulation and anxiety, an evil conscience best knows it.

As iron put into the fire loseth its rust, and becometh clearly red hot, so he that wholly turneth himself unto God, puts off all slothfulness, and is transformed into a new man.

3. When a man beginneth to grow lukewarm, then he is afraid of a little labor, and willingly receiveth external comfort.

But when he once beginneth to overcome himself perfectly, and to walk manfully in the way of God, then he esteemeth those things to be light, which before seemed grievous unto him.

---

[1]Rom. 1:20   [2]Prov. 3:3-4; Psalm 119:100

CHAPTER 5

Of the Consideration of One's Self

We can not trust ourselves too much,[1] because grace oftentimes is lacking in us, and understanding also.

There is but little light in us, and that which we have we quickly lose by our negligence.

Oftentimes too we do not perceive our own inward blindness.

We often do evil, and do worse[2] in excusing ourselves.

We are sometimes moved with passion, and we think it to be zeal.

We reprehend small things in others, and pass over greater matters in ourselves.[3]

We quickly enough feel and weigh what we suffer at the hands of others; but we mind not what others suffer from us.

He that doth well and rightly consider his own works, will find little cause to judge hardly of another.

2. The inward Christian preferreth the care of himself before all other cares.[4] And he that diligently attendeth unto himself, doth seldom speak much of others.

Thou wilt never be so inwardly devout,

---

[1] Jer. 17:5   [2] Psalm 141:4
[3] Matt. 7:5   [4] Matt. 16:26

unless thou pass over other men's affairs with silence, and look especially to thyself.

If thou attend wholly unto God and thyself, thou wilt be but little moved with whatsoever thou seest outside.[5]

Where art thou, when thou art not with thyself? And when thou hast overrun all things, what hast thou then profited, if thou hast neglected thyself?

If thou desirest peace of mind and true unity of purpose, thou must still put all things behind thee, and look only upon thyself.

3. Thou shalt then make great progress, if thou keep thyself free from all temporal care.

Thou shalt greatly fall back, if thou esteem anything temporal as of value.

Let nothing be great unto thee, nothing high, nothing pleasing, nothing acceptable, but only God himself, or that which is of God.

Consider all comfort vain,[6] which thou receivest from any creature.

A soul that loveth God, despiseth all things that are inferior unto God.

God alone is everlasting, and of infinite greatness, filling all creatures; the soul's solace, and the true joy of the heart.

[5] 1 Cor. 4:3; Gal. 1:10   [6] Eccles. 1:14

CHAPTER 6

Of the Joy of a Good Conscience

The glory of a good man is the testimony of a good conscience.[1]

Have a good conscience, and thou shalt ever have joy.

A good conscience is able to bear very much, and is very cheerful in adversities.

An evil conscience is always fearful and unquiet.[2]

Thou shalt rest sweetly, if thy heart do not condemn thee.

Never rejoice but when thou hast done well.

Sinners have never true joy, nor feel inward peace; because "there is no peace for the wicked," saith the Lord.[3]

If they should say, "We are in peace, no evil shall fall upon us,[4] and who shall dare to hurt us?" believe them not; for upon a sudden will arise the wrath of God, and their deeds shall be brought to naught, and their thoughts shall perish.

2. To glory in tribulation, is no hard thing for him that loveth: for so to glory, is to glory in the cross of the Lord.[5]

That glory is short which is given and received from men.[6]

---

[1]1 Cor. 1:31
[2]Wisd. 17:11
[3]Isaiah 57:21
[4]Luke 12:19
[5]Rom. 8 [perhaps 5:3]; Gal. 6:14
[6]John 5:44

Sorrow always accompanieth the world's glory.

The glory of the good is in their consciences, and not in the mouths of men. The gladness of the just is of God,[7] and in God; and their joy is of the truth.

He that desireth true and everlasting glory, careth not for that which is temporal.

And he that seeketh temporal glory, or despises it not from his heart, showeth himself but little to love the glory of Heaven.

He enjoyeth great tranquillity of mind, that careth neither for the praises nor dispraises of men.

3. He will easily be content and pacified, whose conscience is pure.

Thou art not the more holy, though thou be praised; nor the more worthless, though thou be dispraised.

What thou art, that thou art; neither canst thou be said to be greater than what thou art in the sight of God.

If thou consider what thou art within thee, thou wilt not care what men say of thee.

Man looketh on the countenance, but God on the heart.[8] Man considereth the deeds, but God weigheth the intentions.

To be always doing well, and to esteem little of himself, is the sign of an humble soul.

---

[7] 2 Cor. 3:5   [8] 1 Sam. 16:7

Not to look for comfort by any creature, is a sign of great purity and inward confidence.

4. He that seeketh no witness for himself from without, doth show that he hath wholly committed himself unto God.

"For not he that commendeth himself, the same is approved," saith Paul, "but whom God commendeth."[9]

To walk inwardly with God, and not to be kept by any outward affection, is the state of a spiritual man.

CHAPTER 7

Of the Love of Jesus Above All Things

Blessed is he that understandeth[1] what it is to love Jesus, and to despise himself for Jesus's sake.

Thou oughtest to leave thy beloved, for thy Beloved;[2] for Jesus will be loved alone above all things.

The love of things created is deceitful and inconstant; the love of Jesus is faithful and lasting.

He that cleaveth unto creatures, shall fall

---

[9]2 Cor. 10:18   [1]Psalm 119:1-2
[2]Deut. 6:5; Matt. 22:37

with that which is frail; he that embraceth Jesus, shall stand firmly for ever.

Love Him and keep Him for thy friend, who, when all go away, will not forsake thee, nor suffer thee to perish in the end.

Thou must someday be separated from all, whether thou wilt or no.

2. Keep close to Jesus both in life and in death, and commit thyself unto His trust, who, when all fail, can alone help thee.

Thy beloved is of such a nature, that he will admit of no rival; but will have thy heart alone, and sit on his own throne as King.

If thou couldest free thyself perfectly from all creatures, Jesus would willingly dwell with thee.

Whatsoever thou reposest in men, outside of Jesus, is all little better than lost.

Trust not nor lean upon a reed blown by the wind; for that all flesh is grass, and all the glory thereof shall wither away as the flower of the field.[3]

3. Thou shalt quickly be deceived, if thou only look to the outward appearance of men.

For if in them thou seekest thy comfort and gain, thou shalt too often feel loss.

If thou seekest Jesus in all things, thou shalt surely find Jesus.

But if thou seekest thyself, thou shalt also find thyself, but to thine own harm.

---

[3] Isaiah 40:6

For man doth more hurt himself if he seek not Jesus, than the whole world and all his adversaries.

CHAPTER 8

Of Familiar Converse With Jesus

When Jesus is present, all is well, and nothing seems difficult; but when Jesus is absent, everything is hard.

When Jesus speaks not inwardly to us, all other comfort is without value; but if Jesus speak but one word, we feel great consolation.

Did not Mary Magdalene rise immediately from the place where she wept, when Martha said to her, "The Master is come, and calleth for thee?"[1]

Happy hour, when Jesus calleth from tears to spiritual joy!

How dry and hard art thou without Jesus! How foolish and vain, if thou desire anything out of Jesus!

Is not this a greater loss, than if thou shouldest lose the whole world?[2]

2. What can the world profit thee without Jesus?

To be without Jesus is a grievous hell; and to be with Jesus, a sweet paradise.

---

[1]John 11:28   [2]Matt. 16:26

If Jesus be with thee, no enemy shall be able to hurt thee.[3]

He that findeth Jesus, findeth a good treasure,[4] yea, a Good above all good.

And he that loseth Jesus, loseth much indeed, yea, more than the whole world!

Most poor is he who liveth without Jesus;[5] and he most rich who is well with Jesus.

3. It is matter of great art to know how to hold converse with Jesus: and to know how to keep Jesus, a point of great wisdom.

Be thou humble and peaceable, and Jesus will be with thee.[6]

Be devout and quiet, and Jesus will stay with thee.

Thou mayest soon drive away Jesus, and lose his favor, if thou wilt turn to outward things.

And if thou shouldest drive him from thee, and lose him, unto whom wilt thou flee, and whom wilt thou then seek for thy friend?

Without a friend thou canst not well live; and if Jesus be not above all a friend to thee, thou shalt be indeed sad and desolate.

Thou actest therefore like a fool, if thou trust or rejoice in any other.[7]

It is preferable to have all the world against us, rather than to have Jesus offended with us.

Among all therefore that be dear unto us, let Jesus alone be specially beloved.

---

[3]Matt. 13:44   [4]Rom. 8:35   [5]Luke 12:21
[6]Prov. 3:17   [7]Gal. 6:14

4. Love all for Jesus, but Jesus for himself.

Jesus Christ alone is especially to be beloved; who alone is found good and faithful above all friends.

For him, and in him, let as well friends as foes be dear unto thee; and all these are to be prayed for, that they all may know and love him.[8]

Never desire to be especially commended or beloved, for that appertaineth only unto God, who hath none like unto himself.

Neither do thou desire that the heart of any should be set on thee, nor do thou set thy heart on the love of any; but let Jesus be in thee, and in every good man.

5. Be pure and free within, and entangle not thy heart with any creature.

Thou oughtest to be naked and open before God, ever carrying thy heart pure toward him, if thou wouldest be free to consider and see how sweet the Lord is.

And truly unless thou be prevented and drawn by his grace, thou shalt never attain to that happiness to forsake and cast off all, that thou alone mayest be united to him alone.

For when the grace of God cometh unto a man, then he is made able to do all things. And when it goeth away, then is he poor and weak, and as it were left only for the lash and beating.

In this case thou oughtest not to be dejected,

---

[8]Matt. 5:44; Luke 6:27-28

not to despair; but in God's will to rest steadily, and whatever comes upon thee, to endure it for the glory of Jesus Christ; for after winter followeth summer, after night the day returneth, and after a tempest a great calm.

CHAPTER 9

Of the Want of All Comfort

It is no hard matter to despise human comfort, when we have divine.

It is a very great thing to be able to want both human and divine comfort;[1] and, for God's honor, to be willing cheerfully to endure banishment of heart; and to seek one's self in nothing, nor to regard his own merit.

What great matter is it, if at the coming of grace thou be cheerful and devout? this hour is wished for of all men.

He rideth easily enough whom the grace of God carrieth.

And what marvel if he feel not his burden, who is borne up by the Almighty, and led by the sovereign Guide?

2. We are always willing to have something for our comfort; and a man doth not without difficulty put off and forsake himself.

---

[1] Phil. 2:12

The holy martyr Laurence with his priest, overcame the world, because whatsoever seemed delightful in the world he despised; and for the love of Christ he patiently suffered God's chief priest Sixtus, whom he most dearly loved, to be even taken away from him.

He therefore conquered the love of man by the love of the Creator; and he rather chose what pleased God, than human comfort.

Do thou also learn to part with even a near and dear friend, for the love of God.

Nor take it hard, when thou art deserted by a friend, as knowing that we all at last must be separated one from another.

3. A man must strive long and mightily within himself, before he can learn fully to master himself, and to draw his whole heart into God.

When a man trusteth in himself, he easily inclines toward human comforts.

But a true lover of Christ, and a diligent seeker of virtue, does not fall back on comforts, nor seek such sensible sweetnesses; but rather prefers hard exercises, and to sustain severe labors for Christ.

4. When therefore spiritual comfort is given thee from God, receive it with thankfulness; but understand that it is the gift of God, not any merit of thine.

Be not puffed up, be not too joyful nor vainly presumptuous; but rather be the more humble for that gift, more wary too and fearful in all thine actions; for that hour will pass away, and temptation will follow.

When comfort is taken from thee, do not immediately despair; but with humility and patience wait for the heavenly visitation; for God is able to give thee back again more ample comfort.

This is nothing new nor strange to them that have experience in the way of God: for the great saints and ancient prophets had oftentimes experience of such kind of vicissitudes.

5. For which cause, one under the enjoyment of divine grace[2] said, "I said in my prosperity I shall never be moved."

But when grace had departed, what he found in himself he goes on thus to speak of: "Thou didst turn thy face from me, and I was troubled."

Yet in the midst of all this he doth not despair, but more earnestly prayeth unto the Lord, and saith, "Unto Thee, O Lord, will I cry, and I will pray unto my God."

At length he receives the fruit of his prayer, and testifies that he was heard, saying, "The Lord hath heard me, and taken pity on me; the Lord is become my helper."

But wherein? "Thou hast turned," saith he, "my sorrow into joy, and Thou hast compassed me about with gladness."

If great saints were so dealt with, we that are

---

[2] Psalm 30:6-11

weak and poor ought not to despair, if we be sometimes fervent and sometimes cold; for the Spirit cometh and goeth, according to the good pleasure of his own will.[3] For which cause blessed Job saith, "Thou visitest him early in the morning, and suddenly Thou provest him."[4]

6. Whereupon then can I hope, or wherein ought I to trust, but in the great mercy of God alone, and in the only hope of heavenly grace?

For whether I have with me good men, either religious brethren, or faithful friends; whether holy books, or beautiful treatises, or sweet chanting and hymns, all these help but little, and have but little savor, when grace forsaketh me, and I am left in mine own poverty.

At such time there is no better remedy than patience, and the denying of myself according to the will of God.[5]

7. I never found any so religious and devout, that he had not sometimes a withdrawing of grace, or felt not some decrease of zeal.

There was never saint so highly rapt and illuminated, who first or last was not tempted.

For he is not worthy of the high contemplation of God, who hath not been exercised with some tribulation for God's sake.

For temptation going before, is wont to be a sign of ensuing comfort.

For unto those that are proved by temptations, heavenly comfort is promised. "He that

---

[3]John 3:8   [4]Job 7:18   [5]Luke 9:23

shall overcome," saith He, "I will give him to eat of the tree of life."[6]

8. But divine consolation is given, that a man may be stronger to bear adversities.

There followeth also temptation, lest he should grow proud of any good.

The devil sleepeth not,[7] neither is the flesh as yet dead; therefore cease not to prepare thyself for the battle; for on thy right hand and on thy left are enemies who never rest.

CHAPTER 10

Of Gratitude for the Grace of God

Why seekest thou rest, since thou art born to labor?[1]

Dispose thyself to patience, rather than to comfort, and to the bearing of the cross, rather than to gladness.[2]

What worldly man is there that would not willingly receive spiritual joy and comfort, if he could always have it?

For spiritual comforts exceed all the delights of the world and pleasures of the flesh.

For all worldly delights are either vain or unclean; but spiritual delights are only pleasant

---

[6] Rev. 2:7   [7] 1 Pet. 5:8
[1] Job 5:7   [2] Luke 14:27

and honest, sprung from virtue, and infused by God into pure minds.

But no man can always enjoy these divine comforts according to his desire; for the time of temptation is not long away.

2. But false freedom of mind, and great confidence in ourselves, is very contrary to heavenly visitations.

God doth well for us in giving the grace of comfort; but man doth evil in not returning all again unto God with thanksgiving.

And therefore the gifts of grace can not flow in us, because we are unthankful to the Giver, and return them not wholly to the source and fountain.[3]

For grace always attendeth him that is duly thankful; and from the proud shall be taken that which is wont to be given to the humble.

3. I desire not that consolation that taketh from me compunction; nor do I affect that contemplation which leadeth to haughtiness of mind.

For all that is high is not holy: nor all that is sweet, good; nor every desire pure; nor is everything that is dear unto us pleasing to God.

Willingly do I accept that grace, whereby I may ever be found more humble, and more affected with holy fear, and may become more ready to renounce myself.

He that is taught by the gift of grace, and

---

[3]Ecclus. 1:5

schooled by the stroke of the withdrawing thereof, will not dare to attribute any good to himself, but will rather acknowledge himself poor and naked.

Give unto God that which is God's,[4] and ascribe unto thyself that which is thine own; that is, give thanks to God for his grace, and acknowledge that to thyself is to be attributed nothing, but only sin, and the punishment owing to sin.

4. Set thyself always in the lowest place,[5] and the highest shall be given thee; for the highest can not stand without the lowest.

The greatest saints before God are the least in their own judgments; and the more glorious they are, so much the humbler within themselves.

Those that are full of truth and heavenly glory, are not desirous of vain glory.

Those that are firmly settled and grounded in God, can in no way be proud.

And they that ascribe all unto God, what good soever they have received, seek not glory of each other, but wish for that glory which is from God alone; and desire above all things to praise God in himself, and in all the saints; and are always tending to this very thing.

5. Be therefore thankful for the least gift, so shalt thou be worthy to receive greater.

Let the least be unto thee even as the greatest,

---

[4] Matt. 22:21   [5] Luke 14:10

and the most contemptible gift as of especial value.

If thou consider the worth of the Giver, no gift will seem little, or of too mean esteem. For that can not be little which is given by the Most High God.

Yea, if he should give punishment and stripes, it ought to be a matter of thankfulness; because he doth it always for our welfare, whatsoever he permitteth to happen unto us.

He that desireth to keep the grace of God, let him be thankful for grace given, and patient for the taking away thereof; let him pray that it may return; let him be cautious and humble, lest he lose it.

CHAPTER 11

How Few Are the Lovers of the Cross of Jesus

Jesus hath now many lovers of his heavenly kingdom, but few bearers of his cross.

He hath many desirous of comfort, but few of tribulation.

He findeth many companions of his table, but few of his abstinence.

All desire to rejoice with him, few are willing to endure anything for him, or with him.

Many follow Jesus unto the breaking of

bread; but few to the drinking of the cup of his passion.[1]

Many reverence his miracles, few follow the ignominy of his cross.

Many love Jesus so long as adversities do not happen.

Many praise and bless him, so long as they receive comforts from him.

But if Jesus hide himself, and leave them but a little while, they fall either into complaining, or into too much dejection of mind.

2. But they who love Jesus for the sake of Jesus, and not for some special comfort of their own, bless him in all tribulation and anguish of heart, as well as in the state of highest comfort.

And although he should never be willing to give them comfort, they notwithstanding would ever praise him, and wish to be always giving thanks.

3. O, how powerful is the pure love of Jesus, which is mixed with no self-interest, or self-love!

Are not all those to be called mercenary, who are ever seeking comforts?

Do they not show themselves to be rather lovers of themselves than of Christ, who are always thinking of their own profit and advantage?[2]

Where shall one be found who is willing to serve God for naught?

---

[1] Luke 9:14; 22:41-42   [2] Phil. 2:21

4. Rarely is any one found so spiritual as to be stript of the love of all earthly things.

For where is any man to be found that is indeed poor in spirit, and free from all creatures? "From afar, yea, from the ends of the earth, is his value."[3]

If a man should give all his substance, yet it is nothing.

And if he should practice great repentance, still it is little.

And if he should attain to all knowledge, he is still afar off.

And if he should be of great virtue, and very fervent devotion, yet there is much wanting; especially, one thing, which is most necessary for him.

What is that? That leaving all, he forsake himself, and go wholly from himself,[4] and retain nothing out of self-love?

And when he hath done all that is to be done, so far as he knoweth, let him think that he hath done nothing.

5. Let him not reckon that much, which might be much esteemed; but let him pronounce himself to be in truth an unprofitable servant, as the Truth himself saith, "When you shall have done all things that are commanded you, say, we are unprofitable servants."[5]

Then may he be truly poor and naked in

---

[3]Prov. 31:10   [4]Matt. 16:24   [5]Luke 17:10

spirit, and say with the prophet, "I am alone and poor."[6]

Yet no man richer than he, no man more powerful, no man more free: for he can leave himself and all things, and set himself in the lowest place.

CHAPTER 12

Of the King's Highway of the Holy Cross

Unto many this seemeth a hard saying, "Deny thyself, take up thy cross, and follow Jesus."[1]

But much harder will it be to hear that last word, "Depart from me, ye cursed, into everlasting fire."[2]

For they who now willingly hear and follow the word of the cross, shall not then fear[3] the sentence of everlasting damnation.

This sign of the cross shall be in the heaven, when the Lord shall come to judgment.

Then all the servants of the cross, who in their lifetime conformed themselves unto Christ crucified, shall draw near unto Christ the Judge with great confidence.

2. Why therefore fearest thou to take up the cross which leadeth thee to heaven?

In the cross is salvation, in the cross is life, in

---

[6]Psalm 25:16   [1]Matt. 16:24
[2]Matt. 25:41   [3]Psalm 112:7

the cross is protection from our enemies, in the cross is infusion of heavenly sweetness, in the cross is strength of mind, in the cross is joy of spirit, in the cross is the height of virtue, in the cross the perfection of sanctity.

There is no salvation of the soul, nor hope of everlasting life, but in the cross.

Take up therefore thy cross and follow Jesus,[4] and thou shalt enter life everlasting. He went before, bearing his cross,[5] and died for thee on the cross, that thou mayest also bear thy cross and desire to die on the cross.

For if thou be dead with him, thou shalt also live with him. And if thou be his companion in pain, thou shalt be partaker with him also in glory.[6]

3. Behold! in the cross all doth consist, and all lieth in our dying thereon; for there is no other way unto life, and unto true inward peace, but the way of the holy cross, and of daily mortification.

Go where thou wilt, seek whatever thou wilt, thou shalt not find a higher way above, nor a safer way below, than the way of the holy cross.

Dispose and order all things according to thy will and judgment; yet thou shalt ever find, that of necessity thou must suffer somewhat, either willingly, or against thy will, and so thou shalt ever find the cross.

---

[4]Luke 14:27   [5]John 19:17   [6]2 Cor. 1:5

For either thou shalt feel pain in thy body, or in thy soul thou shalt suffer tribulation of spirit.

4. Sometimes thou shalt be forsaken of God, sometimes thou shalt be troubled by thy neighbors; and what is more, oftentimes thou shalt be wearisome to thyself.

Neither canst thou be delivered or eased by any remedy or comfort: but so long as it pleaseth God, thou oughtest to bear it.

For God will have thee learn to suffer tribulation without comfort, and that thou subject thyself wholly to him, and by tribulation become more humble.

No man hath so cordial a feeling of the passion of Christ, as he who hath suffered the like himself.

The cross therefore is always ready, and everywhere waits for thee.

Thou canst not flee it wherever thou runnest; for wherever thou goest, thou carriest thyself with thee, and shalt ever find thyself.

Both above and below, without and within, which way soever thou dost turn thee, everywhere thou shalt find the cross; and everywhere of necessity thou must have patience, if thou wilt have inward peace, and enjoy an everlasting crown.

5. If thou bear the cross cheerfully, it will bear thee, and lead thee to the desired end, namely, where there shall be an end of suffering, though here there shall not be.

If thou bear it unwillingly, thou makest for

thyself a new burden, and increasest thy load, and yet notwithstanding thou must bear it.

If thou cast away one cross, without doubt thou shalt find another, and that perhaps a heavier one.

6. Thinkest thou to escape that which no mortal man could ever avoid? Which of the saints in the world was without crosses and tribulation?

For not even our Lord Jesus Christ was ever one hour without the anguish of his passion, so long as he lived. "Christ," saith he, "must needs suffer, and rise again from the dead, and so enter into his glory."[7] And how dost thou seek any other way than this royal way, which is the way of the holy cross?

7. Christ's whole life was a cross and martyrdom; and dost thou seek rest and joy for thyself?

Thou art deceived, thou art deceived, if thou seek any other thing than to suffer tribulations; for this whole mortal life is full of miseries,[8] and signed on every side with crosses.

And the higher a person hath advanced in spirit, so much the heavier crosses he oftentimes findeth; because the grief of his banishment increases with his love to God.

8. Nevertheless, this man, though so many ways afflicted, is not without refreshing comfort, for that he perceiveth very much benefit to accrue unto him by the bearing of his own cross.

---

[7]Luke 24:26   [8]Job 7:1

For whilst he willingly putteth himself under it, all the burden of tribulation is turned into the confidence of divine comfort.

And the more the flesh is wasted by affliction, so much the more is the spirit strengthened by inward grace.

And sometimes he is so comforted with the desire of tribulation and adversity, for the love of conformity to the cross of Christ, that he would not wish to be without grief and tribulation;[9] because he believes that he shall be unto God so much the more acceptable, the more and heavier things he can suffer for him.

This is not the power of man, but it is the grace of Christ, which can and doth so much in weak flesh; so that what naturally it always hates and flees from, that by fervor of spirit, it encounters and loves.

9. It is not according to man's inclination to bear the cross, to love the cross, to chastise the body, and bring it into subjection, to flee honors, willingly to suffer reproaches, to despise himself and to wish to be despised, to endure all adversities and damages, and to desire no prosperity in this world.

If thou look to thyself, thou shalt be able of thyself to accomplish nothing of this kind.[10]

But if thou trust in the Lord, fortitude shall be given thee from heaven, and the world and the flesh shall be made subject to thy command.

---

[9] 2 Cor. 4:16; 11:23-30   [10] 2 Cor. 3:5

Neither shalt thou fear thy enemy the devil, if thou be armed with faith, and signed with the cross of Christ.

10. Set thyself, therefore, like a good and faithful servant of Christ, to bear manfully the cross of thy Lord, who was crucified for thee out of love.

Prepare thyself to bear many adversities and various kinds of troubles in this miserable life; for so it will be with thee, wherever thou art, and so surely thou shalt find it wherever thou hide thyself.

So it must be; nor is there any remedy or means to escape from tribulation and sorrow, but only to endure thyself.

Drink of the lord's cup[11] heartily, if thou desire to be his friend, and to have part with him. As for consolations, leave them to God; let him do therein as shall best please him.

But do thou set thyself to suffer tribulations, and account them the greatest comforts; for the sufferings of this present time, although thou alone couldest suffer them all, can not worthily deserve the glory which is to come.

11. When thou shalt come to this estate, that tribulation[12] shall seem sweet, and thou shalt relish it for Christ's sake; then think it to be well with thee, for thou hast found a paradise upon earth.

As long as it is hard to thee to suffer, and that

---

[11]Matt. 20:23; John 18:11   [12]Rom. 5:3; Gal. 6:14

thou desirest to flee it, so long shalt thou be ill at ease, and the desire to flee from tribulation will follow thee everywhere.

12. If thou dost set thyself to that which thou ought to do, namely, to suffering and to death, it will quickly be better with thee, and thou shalt find peace.

Although thou shouldest have been carried up to the third heaven with Paul,[13] thou art not by this secured that thou shalt suffer no evil. "I will show him," saith Jesus, "how great things he must suffer for my name."[14]

Thou shalt still suffer, if it please thee to love Jesus, and to serve him perpetually.

13. O that thou wert worthy to suffer something for the name of Jesus![15] How great glory would remain unto thyself; what joy would arise to all God's saints; how great edification also to thy neighbor!

For all men commend patience; few, however, they are, who are willing to suffer.

With great reason oughtest thou cheerfully to suffer a little for Christ's sake; since many suffer more grievous things for the world.

14. Know for certain that thou oughtest to lead a dying life.[16] And the more any man dieth to himself, so much the more doth he begin to live unto God.

No man is fit to comprehend things heavenly

---

[13] 2 Cor. 12:4 [14] Acts 9:16
[15] Acts 5:4 [16] Psalm 44:22

unless he submit himself to the bearing of adversities for Christ's sake.

Nothing is more acceptable to God, nothing more wholesome to thee in this world, than to suffer cheerfully for Christ.

And if thou couldest choose thou oughtest rather to wish to suffer adversities for Christ, than to be refreshed with many consolations; because thou wouldest thus be more like unto Christ, and more conformable to all the saints.

For our worthiness, and the proficiency of our spiritual estate, consisteth not in many delights and comforts; but rather in thoroughly enduring great afflictions and tribulations.

15. If there had been any better thing, and more profitable to the salvation of man, than suffering, surely Christ would have showed it by word and example.

For both the disciples that followed him, and also all who desire to follow him, he plainly exhorteth to the bearing of the cross, and saith, "If any will come after me, let him deny himself and take up his cross, and follow me."[17]

So that when we have thoroughly read and searched all, let this be the final conclusion, "that through many tribulations we must enter into the kingdom of God."[18]

---

[17]Luke 9:23   [18]Acts. 14:22

THE THIRD BOOK

Of Internal Consolation

CHAPTER 1

Of Christ Speaking Inwardly to the Faithful Soul

"I will hear what the Lord God will speak in me."[1]

Blessed is the soul which heareth the Lord speaking within her,[2] and receiveth from his mouth the word of consolation.

Blessed are the ears that gladly receive the pulses of the divine whisper,[3] and give no heed to the many whisperings of this world.

Blessed indeed are those ears which hearken not to the voice which is sounding without, but unto the truth teaching inwardly.

Blessed are the eyes which are shut to outward things, but intent on inward things.

Blessed are they that enter far into things internal, and endeavor to prepare themselves more and more, by daily exercises, for the receiving of heavenly secrets.

Blessed are they who are glad to have time to

---

[1]Psalm 85:8   [2]1 Sam. 3:9   [3]Matt. 13:16-17

[125]

spare for God, and shake off all worldly impediments.

2. Consider these things, O my soul, and shut up the door of thy sensual desires, that thou mayest hear what the Lord thy God shall speak in thee.[4]

Thus saith thy Beloved: "I am thy salvation,[5] thy peace, and thy life: keep thyself with me, and thou shalt find peace.

Let go all transitory things, and seek those that be everlasting.

What are all temporal things but seducing snares? and what can all creatures avail thee, if thou be forsaken by the Creator?

Cast off all things temporal, and labor to please thy Creator, and to be faithful unto him, that thou mayest be able to attain unto the true blessedness.

CHAPTER 2

That the Truth Speaketh Inwardly Without Noise of Words

Speak, O Lord, for thy servant heareth.[1]

I am thy servant, grant me understanding, that I may know thy testimonies.[2]

---

[4] Psalm 85:8   [5] Psalm 35:3
[1] 1 Sam. 3:9   [2] Psalm 119:125

Incline my heart to the words of thy mouth: let thy speech distil as the dew.

The children of Israel in times past said unto Moses, "Speak thou unto us, and we will hear: let not the Lord speak unto us, lest we die."[3]

Not so, Lord, not so, I beseech thee: but rather with the prophet Samuel, I humbly and earnestly entreat, "Speak, Lord, for thy servant heareth."

Let not Moses speak unto me, nor any of the prophets, but rather do thou speak, O Lord God, the Inspirer and Enlightener of all the prophets; for thou alone without them canst perfectly instruct me, but they without thee can profit nothing.

2. They indeed may sound forth words, but they can not give the Spirit.

Most beautifully do they speak, but if thou be silent, they cannot inflame the heart.

They teach the letter, but thou openest the sense: they bring forth mysteries, but thou unlockest the meaning of sealed things.

They declare thy commandments, but thou helpest us to fulfil them.

They point out the way, but thou givest strength to walk in it.

What they can do is only outward, but thou instructest and enlightenest the heart.

They water outwardly, but thou givest fruitfulness.

---

[3]Exodus 20:19

They cry aloud in words, but thou impartest understanding to the hearing.

3. Let not Moses therefore speak unto me, but thou O Lord my God, the everlasting truth; lest I die, and prove unfruitful, if I be only warned outwardly, and not inflamed within.

Lest it turn to my condemnation,—the word heard and not fulfilled, known and not loved, believed and not observed.

Speak therefore, Lord, for thy servant heareth; for thou hast the words of eternal life.[4]

Speak thou unto me, to the comfort, however imperfect, of my soul, and to the amendment of my whole life, and to thy praise, and glory, and honor, everlasting.

CHAPTER 3

That the Words of God Are to Be Heard With Humility, and That Many Weigh Them Not

My son, hear my words, words of greatest sweetness, surpassing all the learning of the philosophers and wise men of this world.

"My words are spirit and life,[1] and not to be weighed by the understanding of man.

"They are not to be drawn forth for vain approbation, but to be heard in silence, and to

---

[4] John 6:68   [1] John 6:63

be received with all humility and great affection."

And I said, "Blessed is the man whom thou shalt instruct, O Lord, and shalt teach out of thy law, that thou mayest give him rest from the evil days,[2] and that he be not desolate upon earth."

2. "I taught the prophets from the beginning,"[3] saith the Lord, "and cease not, even to this day, to speak to all; but many are hardened, and deaf to my voice."

Most people do more willingly listen to the world than to God; and sooner follow the desires of their own flesh, than God's good pleasure.

The world promiseth things temporal and mean, and is served with great eagerness: I promise things most high and eternal, and yet the hearts of men are not receptive.

"Who in all things serveth and obeyeth me with so great care as the world and its lords are served withal? "Be ashamed, O Sidon, saith the sea.[4] And if thou ask the cause, hear wherefore.

"For a small income, a long journey is undertaken; for everlasting life, many will scarce once lift a foot from the ground.

"The most pitiful reward is sought after; for a single bit of money sometimes there is shameful contention; for a vain matter and slight promise, men fear not to toil day and night.

"3. But, alas! for an unchangeable good, for

---

[2]Psalm 94:12-13   [3]Heb. 1:1   [4]Isaiah 23:4

an inestimable reward, for the highest honor, and glory without end, they grudge even a little fatigue.

"Be ashamed, therefore, thou slothful and complaining servant, that they are found to be more ready to destruction than thou to life.

"They rejoice more in vanity than thou dost in the truth.

"Sometimes, indeed, they are frustrated of their hope; but My promise deceiveth none,[5] nor sendeth him away empty that trusteth in Me.

"What I have promised, I will give; what I have said I will make good, if only any man remain faithful in My love even to the end.

"I am the Rewarder of all good men,[6] and the strong Approver of all who are devoted to Me.

"4. Write thou My words in thy heart, and meditate diligently on them; for in time of temptation they will be very necessary for thee.

"What thou understandest not when thou readest, thou shalt know in the day of visitation.

"In two ways I am accustomed to visit Mine elect, namely, with temptation and with consolation.

"And I daily read two lessons to them, one in rebuke of their vices, and the other in exhorting them to the increase of their virtues.

---

[5] Rom. 1:16; Matt. 24:35
[6] Rev. 2:23; Matt. 5:6; 25:21

"He that hath My words and despiseth them,
hath One that shall judge him at the last day."

5. *A prayer to implore the grace of devotion*

O Lord, my God! thou art to me whatsoever
is good. And who am I, that I should dare speak
to thee?[7] I am thy poorest, meanest servant, and
a most vile person, much poorer and contemptible than I can or dare express.

Yet do thou remember me, O Lord, because I
am nothing, I have nothing, I can do nothing.

Thou alone art good, just, and holy; thou
canst do all things, thou accomplishest all
things, thou fillest all things, only the sinner
thou leavest empty.

Remember thy mercies, and fill my heart
with thy grace, thou who wilt not that thy
works should be void and in vain.

6. How can I bear up myself in this miserable life, unless thou strengthen me with thy
mercy and grace?

Turn not thy face away from me;[8] delay not
thy visitation; withdraw not thy consolation,
lest my soul become as a thirsty land unto thee.

Teach me, O Lord, to do thy will;[9] teach me
to live worthily and humbly in thy sight; for
thou art my wisdom, thou dost truly know me,
and didst know me before the world was made,
and before I was born in the world.

---

[7]Gen. 18:27; 1 Sam. 18:18, 23
[8]Psalm 69:17   [9]Psalm 143:10

CHAPTER 4

That We Ought to Live in Truth and Humility Before God

My son, walk thou before Me in truth, and ever seek me in simplicity of thy heart.[1]

He that walketh before me in truth, shall be defended from evil assaults, and the truth shall set him[2] free from seducers, and from the slanders of wicked men.

If the truth shall have made thee free, thou shalt be free indeed, and shalt not care for the vain words of men.

O Lord, it is true. According as thou saidst, so I beseech thee, let it be with me; let thy truth teach me, guard me, and preserve me safe to the end.

Let it set me free from all evil affection and inordinate love; and I shall walk with thee in great liberty of heart.

2. I will teach thee (saith the Truth) those things which are right and pleasing in my sight.

Reflect on thy sins with great displeasure and grief, and never esteem thyself anything because of good works.

In truth thou art a sinner; thou art subject to and entangled in many passions. Of thyself thou always tendest to nothing; speedily art thou cast down, speedily overcome, speedily disordered, speedily dissolved.

Gen. 17:1; Wisd. 1:1   [2]John 8:32

Thou hast nothing of which thou canst glory,[3] but many things for which thou oughtest to account thyself vile; for thou art much weaker than thou art able to comprehend.

3. And therefore let nothing seem great unto thee whatsoever thou doest.

Let nothing seem important, nothing precious and wonderful, nothing worthy of esteem, nothing high, nothing truly commendable and to be desired, but that alone which is eternal.

Let the eternal truth be above all things pleasing to thee. Let thy own extreme unworthiness be always displeasing to thee.

Fear nothing, blame nothing, flee nothing, so much as thy faults and sins; which ought to be more unpleasing to thee than any losses whatsoever of earthly goods.

Some walk not sincerely in My sight,[4] but led by a certain curiosity and pride, wish to know my secrets, and to understand the high things of God, neglecting themselves and their own salvation.

These oftentimes, when I resist them, for their pride and curiosity do fall into great temptations and sins.

4. Fear thou the judgments of God, and dread the wrath of the Almighty. Do not, however, discuss the works of the Most High, but search diligently thine own iniquities, in

---

[3] 1 Cor. 4:7   [4] Ecclus. 3:21-23; 2 Cor. 2:17

how great things thou hast offended, and how many good things thou hast neglected.

Some carry their devotion only in books, some in pictures, some in outward signs and figures.

Some have Me in their mouths, but little in their hearts.[5]

Others there are who, being illuminated in their understandings, and purged in their affection, do always long after things eternal, are unwilling to hear of the things of this world, and do serve the necessities of nature with grief; and these perceive what the Spirit of Truth speaketh in them.[6]

For he teacheth them to despise earthly, and to love heavenly things; to neglect the world, and to desire heaven all the day and night.[7]

CHAPTER 5

Of the Wonderful Effect of Divine Love

I praise thee, O Heavenly Father, Father of my Lord Jesus Christ, for that thou hast promised to remember me a poor creature.

O Father of mercies and God of all comfort,[1] thanks be unto thee, who sometimes with thy

---

[5]Isaiah 29:13   [6]Psalm 25:5
[7]Psalm 1:2   [1]2 Cor. 1:3

comfort refreshest me, unworthy as I am of all comfort.

I will always bless and glorify thee, with thy only-begotten Son, and the Holy Ghost, the Comforter, for ever and ever.

Ah, Lord God, thou Holy Lover of my soul, when thou comest into my heart, all that is within me shall rejoice.

Thou art my glory, and the exultation of my heart; thou art my hope and refuge in the day of my trouble.[2]

2. But because I am as yet weak in love, and imperfect in virtue, I have need to be strengthened and comforted by thee; visit me therefore often, and instruct me with all holy discipline.

Set me free from evil passions, and heal my heart of all inordinate affections; that being inwardly cured and thoroughly cleansed, I may be made fit to love, courageous to suffer, steady to persevere.

3. Love is a great thing, yea, great and thorough good; by itself it makes everything that is heavy, light; and it bears evenly all that is uneven.

For it carries a burden which is no burden,[3] and makes everything that is bitter, sweet and tasteful.

The noble love of Jesus impels a man to do great things, and impels him to be always longing for what is more perfect.

---

[2]Psalm 32:7; 59:16   [3]Matt. 11:30

Love desires to be lifted up, and will not be kept back by anything low and mean.

Love desires to be free, and separated from all worldly affections, that so its inward sight may not be hindered; that it may not be entangled by any temporal prosperity, or by any adversity conquered.

Nothing is sweeter than love nothing more courageous, nothing higher, nothing wider, nothing more pleasant, nothing fuller nor better in heaven and earth: because love is born of God, and can not rest but in God, above all created things.

4. He that loveth, flieth, runneth, and rejoiceth; he is free, and can not be restrained.

He giveth all for all, and hath all in all; because he resteth in One highest above all things, from whom all that is good flows and proceeds.

He respecteth not the gifts, but turneth himself above all goods unto the Giver.

Love oftentimes knoweth no measure, but is fervent beyond all measure.

Love feels no burden, thinks nothing of trouble, attempts what is above its strength, complains not of impossibility; for it thinks all things lawful for itself, and all things possible.

It is therefore able to undertake all things, and it completes many things, and causes them to take effect, where he who does not love, would faint and lie down.

5. Love is watchful, and sleeping slumbereth not.[4]

Being weary, it is not tired; being pressed, is not straitened; being alarmed, is not confused; but as a lively flame and burning torch, forces its way upward, and securely passes through all.

If any man love, he knoweth what is the cry of this voice. For it is a loud cry in the ears of God, the mere ardent affection of the soul, when it saith, My God, my Love, thou art all mine, and I all thine.

6. Enlarge thou me in love, that with the inward mouth of my heart I may taste how sweet it is to love, and to be dissolved, and to bathe myself in thy love.

Let me be possessed by love, mounting up above myself, through excess of fervor and admiration.

Let me sing the song of love, let me follow thee, my Beloved, on high; let my soul lose itself in thy praise, rejoicing through love.

Let me love thee more than myself, nor love myself but for thee; and in thee all that truly love thee, as the law of love commandeth, shining out from thyself.

7. Love is swift, sincere, affectionate, pleasant, and amiable; courageous, patient, faithful, prudent, long-suffering, manly, and never seeking itself.[5]

---

[4]Rom. 8:19   [5]1 Cor. 13:5

For in whatever circumstance a person seeketh himself, there he falleth from love.[6]

Love is circumspect, humble, and upright; not yielding to softness or levity, nor attending to vain things; but sober, chaste, steady, quiet, and guarded in all the senses.

Love is submissive and obedient to its superiors, to itself mean and abject, unto God devout and thankful, trusting and hoping always in him, even then when God imparteth no sweetness unto it; for without sorrow none liveth in love.

8. He that is not prepared to suffer all things, and to stand to the will of his Beloved, is not worthy to be called a lover of God.[7]

A lover ought to embrace willingly all that is hard and distasteful, for the sake of his Beloved; and not to turn away from him for any contrary occurrences.

CHAPTER 6

Of the Proof of a True Lover of Christ

My son, thou art not yet a courageous and considerate lover.

Wherefore, O Lord?

Because for a slight opposition thou leavest off thy undertakings, and too eagerly seekest consolation.

---

[6]1 Cor. 10:33; Phil. 2:21   [7]Rom. 8:35

A courageous lover standeth firm in temptations, and believeth not the crafty persuasions of the enemy. As I please him in prosperity, so in adversity I am not unpleasant to him.[1]

2. A prudent lover regardeth not so much the gift of Him who loves him, as the love of the Giver.

He esteems the good will rather than the value of the gift, and sets all gifts below Him whom he loves.

A noble-minded lover resteth not in the gift, but in Me above every gift.

All therefore is not lost, if sometimes thou hast less feeling for Me or my saints than thou wouldest.

That good and sweet affection which thou sometimes feelest, is the effect of grace present, and a sort of foretaste of thy heavenly home; but hereon thou must not lean too much, for it comes and goes.

But to strive against evil motions of the mind which arise, and to reject[2] with scorn the suggestions of the devil, is a notable sign of virtue, and shall have great reward.

3. Let no strange fancies therefore trouble thee, which on any subject whatever may crowd into thy mind. Keep to thy purpose, with courage, and an upright intention toward God.

Neither is it an illusion that sometimes thou art suddenly rapt on high, and presently return-

---

[1] Phil. 4:11-13   [2] Matt. 4:10

est again unto the accustomed vanities of thy heart.

For these thou dost rather unwillingly suffer, than commit; and so long as they displease thee, and thou strivest against them, it is matter of reward and no loss.

4. Know that the ancient enemy doth strive by all means to hinder thy longing for good, and to keep thee clear of all devout exercises, particularly from the veneration of God's saints, from the devout commemoration of my passion, from the profitable remembrance of sins, from watchfulness over thine own heart, and from the firm purpose of advancing in virtue.

Many evil thoughts does he suggest to thee, that so he may cause a wearisomeness and horror in thee, to draw thee away from prayer and holy reading.

Humble confession is displeasing unto him; and if he could, he would cause thee to cease from holy communion.

Trust him not, nor care for him, although he should often set snares of deceit to entrap thee.

Blame him when he suggesteth evil and unclean thoughts unto thee; say unto him,

"Away, thou unclean spirit![3] blush, thou miserable wretch! most unclean art thou that bringest such things unto mine ears.

"Depart from me thou wicked deceiver! thou shalt have no part in me: but Jesus shall be with

---

[3]Matt. 4:10; 16:23

me as a valiant Warrior, and thou shalt stand confounded.

"I would rather die, and undergo any torment, than consent to thee.

"Hold thy peace and be silent; I will hear thee no more, though thou shouldst cause me many troubles. 'The Lord is my Light and my Salvation, whom shall I fear?'[4]

"If whole armies should stand together against me, my heart shall not fear. The Lord is my Helper and my Redeemer."

5. Fight like a good soldier:[5] and if thou sometimes fall through frailty, put on greater strength than before, trusting in my more abundant grace; and take great care against vain pleasing of thyself, and of pride.

This brings many into error, and makes them some times fall into blindness almost incurable.

Let the fall of the proud, thus foolishly presuming on themselves, serve thee for a warning, and keep thee always humble.

CHAPTER 7

Of Concealing Grace Under the Guard of Humility

My son, it is more profitable for thee and safer to conceal the grace of devotion; not to lift thyself on high, nor to speak much thereof, or to dwell

---

[4]Psalm 27:1   [5]Psalm 27:14; 1 Tim. 6:12

much thereon; but rather to despise thyself, and to fear it, as given to one unworthy of it.

This affection must not be too earnestly depended upon, for it may be quickly changed to the contrary.

Think when thou hast grace, how miserable and needy thou art wont to be without grace.

Nor is it in this only that thy progress in spiritual life consists, when thou hast the grace of comfort; but rather when with humility, self-denial, and patience, thou endurest the withdrawing thereof; provided thou do not then relax in the exercise of prayer, nor suffer the rest of thy accustomed duties to be at all neglected.

Rather do thou gladly perform what lieth in thee, according to the best of thy power and understanding; and do not wholly neglect thyself because of the dryness or anxiety of mind which thou feelest.

2. For there are many who when they do not succeed, presently become impatient or slothful.

For the way of man is not always in his power,[1] but it belongeth unto God to give, and to comfort when he will, and how much he will, and whom he will; as it shall please him, and no more.

Some unadvised persons, in the grace of a devoted life, have destroyed themselves; because they attempted more than they were able to

---

[1] Jer. 10:23; Rom. 9:16

perform, not weighing the measure of their own weakness, but rather following the desire of their heart, than the judgment of their reason.

And because they presumed on greater matters than was pleasing to God, they therefore quickly lost his grace.

They who had built themselves nests[2] in heaven were made helpless and vile outcasts; to the end that being humbled and impoverished, they might learn not to fly with their own wings, but to trust under my feathers.

They that are yet but novices and inexperienced in the way of the Lord, unless they govern themselves by the counsel of discreet persons, may easily be deceived and broken to pieces.

3. And if they will rather follow their own notions than trust to others who are more experienced, their end will be dangerous, at least if they are unwilling to be drawn away from their own fond conceit.

It is rarely the case that they who are self-wise endure humbly to be governed by others.

Better it is to have a small portion of good sense with humility,[3] and a slender understanding, than great treasures of learning with vain self-complacency.

Better it is for thee to have little than much of that which may make thee proud.

He acts not very discreetly, who wholly gives himself over to joy, forgetting his former

---

[2] Isaiah 14:13   [3] Psalm 16:2; 17:10

helplessness, and that chaste fear of the Lord, which is afraid of losing the grace which hath been offered.

Nor again is he very valiantly wise who in time of adversity or any tribulation, at once yields too much to despairing thoughts, and reflects, and thinks of Me less confidingly than he ought.

4. He who in time of peace is willing to be over secure,[4] shall be often found in time of war too much dejected and full of fears.

If thou hadst the wisdom always to continue humble and moderate within thyself, and also thoroughly to moderate and govern thy spirit, thou wouldest not so quickly fall into danger and offence.

It is good counsel, that when fervor of spirit is kindled within thee, thou shouldest consider how it will be when that light shall leave thee.

And when this does happen, then remember that the light may return again, which as a warning to thyself and for mine own glory, I have withdrawn for a time.[5]

5. Such trials are often more profitable, than if thou shouldst always have things prosper according to thy will.

For a man's worthiness is not to be estimated by the number of visions and consolations which he may have, or by his knowledge of the

---

[4]1 Thess. 5:6   [5]Job 7

Scriptures, or by his being placed in a more elevated station.

But [the proof is] if he be grounded in true humility, and full of divine charity; if he be always purely and sincerely seeking God's honor; if he think nothing of and sincerely despise himself,[6] and even rejoice more to be despised and put low by others, than to be honored by them.

CHAPTER 8

*Of a Mean Conceit of Ourselves
in the Sight of God*

Shall I speak unto my Lord since I am but dust and ashes?[1] If I esteem myself to be anything more, behold, thou standest against me, and my sins bear true witness, and I can not contradict it.

But if I abase myself, and reduce myself to nothing, and draw back from all self-esteem, and reduce myself to dust, thy grace will be favorable to me, and thy light near unto my heart; and all self-esteem, however little, shall be swallowed up in the valley of my nothingness, and perish for ever.

There thou showest thyself unto me, what I am, what I have been, and to what I have come; for I am nothing, and I knew it not.

---

[6]Psalm 85:10   [1]Gen. 18:27

If I be left to myself, behold, I become nothing but mere weakness; but if thou for an instant look upon me, I am forthwith made strong, and am filled with new joy.

And a great wonder it is, that I am so suddenly lifted up, and so graciously embraced by thee, who of mine own weight am always sinking downward.

2. They love is the cause hereof, freely preventing me, and relieving me in so many necessities, guarding me also from pressing dangers, and snatching me from evils innumerable.

For indeed by loving myself perversely, I lost myself;[2] and by seeking thee alone, and purely loving thee, I have found both myself and thee, and by that love have more deeply reduced myself to nothing.

Because thou, O sweetest Lord, dealest with me above all desert, and above all that I dare hope for, or ask.

3. Blessed be thou, my God; for although I be unworthy of all good, yet thy noble bounty and infinite goodness never ceaseth to do good even to the ungrateful,[3] and to those who are turned away far from thee.

Turn thou us unto thee, that we may be thankful, humble, and devout; for thou art our salvation, our courage, and our strength.

---

[2]John 12:25   [3]Matt. 5:45

CHAPTER 9

That All Things Are to Be Referred Unto God, as Their Last End

My son, I ought to be thy supreme and ultimate end, if thou desire to be truly blessed.

Through this intention thy affections will be purified, which are too often inordinately inclined to selfishness and unto created things.

For if in anything thou seekest thyself, immediately thou faintest and becomest barren.

I would therefore thou shouldst refer all things principally unto Me, for I am He who have given all.

Consider everything as flowing from the Highest Good;[1] and therefore unto Me as their Original all must be attributed.

2. From Me, as from a living fountain, the small and the great, the poor and the rich, do draw the water of life;[2] and they that willingly and freely serve Me, shall receive grace for grace.

But he who desires to glory in things other than Me,[3] or to take pleasure in some private good, shall not be established in true joy, nor be enlarged in his heart, but shall many ways be impeded and straitened.

Thou oughtest therefore to ascribe nothing of good to thyself, nor do thou attribute virtue

---

[1] Ecclus. 1:5   [2] John 4:14   [3] 1 Cor. 1:29

unto any man; but give all unto God, without whom man hath nothing.

I have given all,[4] and my will is that all be returned unto Me again; and with great strictness do I require a return of thanks.

3. This is the truth whereby vain glory is put to flight.

And if heavenly grace enter in and true charity, there shall be no envy nor narrowness of heart, neither shall self-love keep possession.

For divine charity overcometh all things, and enlargeth all the powers of the soul.

If thou art truly wise, thou wilt rejoice in Me alone, in Me alone thou wilt hope; for none is good, save God alone,[5] who is to be praised above all things, and in all to be blessed.

CHAPTER 10

That to Despise the World and Serve God
Is a Sweet Life

Now I will speak again, O Lord, and will not be silent; I will say in the hearing of my God, my Lord, and my King, who is on high: "O how great is the abundance of thy goodness, O Lord, which thou hast laid up for those that fear thee."[1]

But what art thou to those who love thee?

---

[4] 1 Cor. 4:7 [5] Matt. 19:17; Luke 18:19 [1] Psalm 31:19

what to those who serve thee with their whole heart?

Truly unspeakable is the sweetness of contemplating thee, which thou bestowest on those that love thee.

In this above all thou hast showed me the sweetness of thy love: that when I was not, thou madest me, when I went far astray from thee, thou broughtest me back again, that I might serve thee, and hast commanded me to love thee.[2]

2. O Fountain of love everlasting, what shall I say concerning thee?

How can I forget thee, who hast promised to remember me, even after I had wasted away and was lost.

Thou hast showed mercy to thy servant beyond all expectation: and hast shown favor and loving-kindness beyond all desert.

What return shall I make to thee for this favor?[3] For it is not granted to all to forsake all, to renounce the world, and to undertake a life of religious devotion.

Is it any great thing that I should serve thee,[4] whom the whole creation is bound to serve?

It ought not to seem much to me to serve thee; but rather this doth appear much to me, and wonderful, that thou hast promised to receive into thy service one so poor and unwor-

---

[2]Gen. 1:27; Psalm 119:73; Matt. 15 [perhaps 10:37]
[3]Psalm 116:12   [4]Judges 16:15

thy, and to make him one with thy beloved servants.

3. Behold, all things are thine which I have, and whereby I serve thee.[5]

And yet contrariwise, thou rather servest me than I thee.

Behold, heaven and earth, which thou hast created for the service of man, are readily prepared, and do daily perform whatever thou hast commanded.

And this is little: thou hast moreover also appointed angels to minister to man.[6]

But that which excelleth all this is, that thou thyself hast consented to serve man, and hast promised that thou wouldest give thyself unto him.

4. What shall I give thee for all these thousands of benefits? I would I could serve thee all the days of my life.

I wish I were able, at least for one day, to do thee some worthy service.

Truly thou art worthy of all service, of all honor, and everlasting praise.

Truly thou art my Lord, and I am thy poor servant, who art bound to serve thee with all my might, neither ought I ever to be weary of praising thee.

And this I wish to do, this I desire: and whatsoever is wanting unto me, do thou, I beseech thee, agree to supply.

---

[5]1 Cor. 4:7   [6]Psalm 91:11; Heb. 1:14

5. It is a great honor, and a great glory, to serve thee and despise all things for thee.

For great grace shall be given to those who shall have willingly subjected themselves to thy most holy service.

They who for thy love shall have cast away all carnal delights, shall find the sweetest consolations of the Holy Spirit.[7]

They shall attain great freedom of mind, who for thy name's sake enter into the narrow way,[8] and have left off all worldly care.

6. O sweet and delightful service of God,[9] by which a man is made truly free and holy!

O sacred state of religious servitude, which makes a man equal to the angels, pleasing to God, terrible to devils, and worthy to be commended by all the faithful!

O welcome service and ever to be desired, in which we are rewarded with the greatest good, and attain to joy which shall never end!

CHAPTER 11

That the Longings and Desires of Our Hearts Are to Be Examined and Moderated

My son, it is needful for thee still to learn many things more, which thou hast not yet well learned.

---

[7]Matt. 19:29   [8]Matt. 7:14   [9]Matt. 11:30; 1 John 5:3

What are these, O Lord?

That thou conform thy desires[1] wholly according to my good pleasure; and that thou be not a lover of thyself, but an earnest follower of my will.

Various longings and desires oftentimes inflame thee, and drive thee forward with vehemence: but do thou consider whether thou be not moved rather for thine own advantage, than for my honor?

If I myself be the cause, thou wilt be well content with whatsoever I shall ordain; but if there lurk in thee any self-seeking,[2] behold, this it is that hindereth thee and weigheth thee down.

2. Take care therefore thou lean not too much upon any preconceived desire, without asking my counsel, lest perhaps afterward thou repent, or be displeased with that which at first pleased thee, and which thou wast earnestly zealous for as being the best.

For not every inclination which seems good is immediately to be followed; nor again is every contrary affection at the first to be avoided.

It is sometimes desirable to use restraint even in good desires and endeavors, lest through too much eagerness thou incur distraction of mind; lest by thy want of self-government thou generate a scandal unto others; or again, being

---

[1]Psalm 108:1; Matt. 6:10   [2]Phil. 2:21

by others thwarted and resisted, thou become suddenly bewildered, and so fall.

3. Sometimes, however, thou must use violence,[3] and resist manfully thy sensual appetite, not regarding what the flesh would or would not;[4] but rather taking pains that even against its will it may be made subject to the Spirit.[5]

And so long ought it to be chastised and to be forced to remain under servitude, until it be prepared for everything, and learn to be content with a little, and to be pleased with plain things, nor to murmur against any inconvenience.

CHAPTER 12

Of the Growth of Patience in the Soul, and of Striving Against Concupiscence

O Lord my God, patience is very necessary for me,[1] as I plainly see, for many adverse things in this life do happen to us.

For whatever plans I shall devise for my own peace, my life can not be without war and sorrow.[2]

It is so, my son. But my will is, that thou

---

[3]Phil. 2:12   [4]Rom. 8:1-13; 2 Cor. 4:10; 10:3
[5]1 Cor. 9:27   [1]Heb. 10:36   [2]Job 7:1

seek not that peace which is free of temptations, or which feeleth nothing adverse: but rather think that thou hast then found peace, when thou art exercised with sundry tribulations[3] and tried in many adversities.

2. If thou say that thou art not able to suffer much, how then wilt thou endure the fire hereafter?

Of two evils the less is always to be chosen.

That thou mayest therefore avoid the future everlasting punishment, endeavor to endure present evils patiently for God's sake.

Dost thou think that the men of this world suffer nothing or but a little? Ask even of those who enjoy the greatest pleasures, and thou shalt find it otherwise.

But thou wilt say, they have many delights, and follow their own wills, and therefore they do not think much of their own afflictions.

Be it so, that they do have whatsoever they will; but how long dost thou think it will last?

3. Behold, the wealthy of this world shall be consumed like smoke,[4] and there shall be no memory of their past joys!

Yea, even while they are yet alive, they rest in them not without bitterness, weariness, and fear.

For from the same thing in which they imagine their delight to be, oftentimes they receive the penalty of sorrow.

---

[3]James 1:2 [4]Psalm 68:2

Nor is it anything but just, that having inordinately sought and followed after pleasures, they should enjoy them not without shame and bitterness.

4. Oh, how brief, how false, how inordinate and filthy, are all those pleasures!

Yet so drunken and blind are men that they understand it not; but like dumb beasts, for the sake of a little enjoyment in this corruptible life, they incur the death of the soul.

Thou therefore, my son, "go not after thy lusts, but refrain thyself from thine appetites."[5] "Delight thyself in the Lord, and he shall give thee the desires of thy heart."[6]

5. For if thou desire true delight, and to be more plentifully comforted by me, behold, in the contempt of all worldly things, and in the cutting off all base delights, shall be thy blessing, and abundant consolation shall be rendered to thee.

And the more thou withdrawest thyself from all solace of creatures, so much the sweeter and more powerful consolations shalt thou find in me.

But at the first, thou shalt not without some sadness, nor without a laborious conflict, attain unto these consolations.

Old inbred habits will make resistance, but by better habits they shall be entirely overcome.

---

[5] Ecclus. 18:30   [6] Psalm 37:4

The flesh will murmur against thee; but with fervency of spirit thou shalt bridle it.

The old serpent will incite and trouble thee, but by prayer he shall be put to flight; also by any useful employment his greater access to thee shall be prevented.

CHAPTER 13

Of the Obedience of One in Humble Subjection, After the Example of Jesus Christ

My son, he that strives to withdraw himself from obedience, withdraweth himself from grace: and he who seeketh for himself particular privileges,[1] loseth those which are common to all.

He that doth not cheerfully and freely submit himself to his superior, it is a sign that his flesh is not as yet perfectly obedient unto him, but oftentimes resisteth and murmureth against him.

Learn thou therefore quickly to submit thyself to thy superior, if thou desire to keep thine own flesh under the yoke.

For more speedily is the outward enemy overcome, if the inward man be not laid low.

There is no worse enemy, nor more trouble-

---

[1] Matt. 16:24

some to the soul, than thou art unto thyself, if thou be not well in harmony with the Spirit.

It is altogether necessary that thou adopt a true contempt for thyself, if thou desire to prevail against flesh and blood.

2. Because as yet thou lovest thyself too inordinately therefore thou art afraid to resign thyself wholly to the will of others.

And yet, what great matter is it,[2] if thou, who art but dust and nothing, subject thyself to a man for God's sake, when I, the Almighty and the Most Highest, who created all things of nothing, humbly subjected myself to man for thy sake?

I became of all men the most humble and the most abject, that thou mightest overcome thy pride with my humility.

O dust, learn to be obedient. Learn to humble thyself, thou earth and clay, and to bow thyself down under the feet of all men.

Learn to break thine own will, and to yield thyself to all subjection.

3. Be fiercely angry against thyself, and suffer no pride to dwell in thee: but show thyself so humble, and so very small, that all may be able to walk over thee, and to tread thee down as the mire of the streets. Vain man, what hast thou to complain of?

What canst thou answer, foul sinner, to them that upbraid thee, thou who hast so often

---

[2] Luke 2:7; John 13:14

offended God, and so many times deserved hell?

But mine eye spared thee, because thy soul was precious in my sight; that thou mightest know my love, and ever be thankful for my favors.

Also that thou mightest continually give thyself to true subjection and humility, and endure patiently any contempt which may be put upon thee.

CHAPTER 14

Of the Duty of Considering the Secret Judgments of God, That So We Be Not Lifted Up for Anything Good in Us

Thou, O Lord, thunderest forth thy judgments over me, thou shakest all my bones with fear and trembling, and my soul is exceedingly afraid.

I stand astonished; and I consider that "the heavens are not pure in thy sight."[1]

If in angels thou didst find wickedness,[2] and didst not spare even them, what shall become of me?

Even stars fell from heaven;[3] what then can I presume who am but dust?

They whose works seemed commendable, have fallen into the lowest misery; and those

---

[1]Job 15:15   [2]Job 4:18   [3]Rev. 8:10

who did eat the bread of angels,[4] I have seen delighting themselves with the husks of swine.

2. There is therefore no sanctity, if thou, O Lord, withdraw thy hand.

No wisdom availeth, if thou cease to govern us.

No courage helpeth, if thou leave off to preserve us.

No chastity is secure, if thou do not protect it.

No custody of our own availeth, if thy sacred watchfulness be not present with us.

For, if we be left to ourselves we sink and perish; but being visited of thee we are raised up and live.

Truly we are unsteadfast, but through thee we are confirmed: we wax cold, but by thee we are inflamed.

3. Oh, how humbly and lowly ought I to think of myself! how ought I to esteem it as nothing, if I should seem to have any good!

With what profound humility ought I to submit myself to thy unfathomable judgments, O Lord; where I find myself to be nothing else but nothing, and still nothing!

O unmeasurable weight! O sea that can never be passed over, where I can discover nothing of myself save only and wholly nothing!

Where then is the lurking-place of glory? where the confidence conceived of virtue?

---

[4]Psalm 78:25

All vain-glorying is swallowed up in the deep of thy judgments over me.

4. What is all flesh in thy sight?

Shall the clay glory against him that formeth it?

How can he be puffed up with vain words, whose heart is truly subject to God?[5]

Not all the world can lift him up, whom the truth hath subjected unto itself; neither shall he, who hath firmly settled his whole hope in God, be moved with the tongues of any who praise him.

For even they themselves who speak, behold, they all are nothing, for they will pass away with the sound of their own words; but the truth of the Lord remaineth for ever.[6]

CHAPTER 15

In Everything Which We Desire, How We Ought to Stand Affected, and What We Ought to Say

My son, say thou thus in everything; "Lord, if this be pleasing unto thee, let it be so.[1]

"Lord, if it be to thy honor, in thy name let this be done.

---

[5]Isaiah 29:16; Ecclus. 23:4-5   [6]Psalm 117:2
[1]James 3 [perhaps 4:15]

"Lord, if thou seest it good, and allowest it to be profitable for me, then grant unto me that I may use this to thine honor.

"But if thou knowest it will be harmful unto me, and no profit to the health of my soul, take away any such desire from me."

For not every desire is of the Holy Spirit, though it seem unto a man right and good.

It is difficult to judge truly whether a good spirit or an evil one drive thee to desire this or that; or whether by thine own spirit thou be moved thereunto.

Many have been deceived in the end, who at the first seemed to be led on by a good spirit.

2. Therefore whatever occurs to the mind as desirable, must always be desired and prayed for in the fear of God, and with humility of heart; and most of all thou must commit the whole matter to me, with special resignation of thyself, and thou must say:

"O Lord, thou knowest what is best for us, let this or that be done, as thou wilt.

"Give what thou wilt, and how much thou wilt, and when thou wilt.

"Deal with me as thou thinkest good, and as best pleaseth thee, and is most for thy honor.

"Set me where thou wilt, and deal with me in all things just as thou wilt.

"I am in thy hand: turn me round, and turn me back again, which way soever thou please.

"Behold, I am thy servant, prepared for all things; for I desire not to live unto myself, but unto thee; and oh that I could do it worthily and perfectly!"

3. *A prayer that the will of God may be fulfilled*

O most merciful Jesus, grant to me thy grace, that it may be with me, and labor with me,[2] and continue with me even to the end.

Grant that I may always desire and will that which is to thee most acceptable and most pleasing.

Let thy will be mine, and let my will ever follow thine, and agree perfectly with it.

Let my willingness or unwillingness be all one with thine, and let me not be able to will or not will anything else, but what thou willest or not willest.

4. Grant that I may die to all things that are in the world, and for thy sake love to be despised, and not known in this world.

Grant to me above all things that can be desired, to rest in thee, and in thee to have my heart at peace.

Thou art the true peace of the heart, thou its only rest; out of thee all things are hard and restless. In this very peace, that is, in thee, the one chiefest eternal Good I will sleep and rest.[3]   Amen.

---

[2]Wisd. 9:10   [3]Psalm 4:8

CHAPTER 16

That True Comfort Is to Be Sought in God Alone

Whatsoever I can desire or imagine for my comfort, I look for it not here but hereafter.

For if I alone should have all the comforts of the world, and might enjoy all the delights thereof,[1] it is certain that they could not long endure.

Wherefore, O my soul, thou canst not be fully comforted,[2] nor have perfect refreshment, but in God, the Comforter of the poor, and Patron of the humble.

Wait a little while, O my soul, wait for the divine promise, and thou shalt have abundance of all good things in heaven.

If thou desire inordinately the things that are present, thou shalt lose the celestial and eternal.

Use temporal things, and desire eternal.

Thou canst not be satisfied with any temporal goods because thou art not created to enjoy them.

2. Although thou shouldst possess all created good, yet couldest thou not be happy thereby, nor blessed; but in God, who created all things, thy whole blessedness and happiness consisteth;[3] not such as is seen and commended by the foolish lovers of the world, but such as

---

[1]Matt. 16:26   [2]Psalm 77:1-2   [3]Wisd. 2:23

the good and faithful servants of Christ wait for, and of which the spiritual and pure in heart, whose conversation is in heaven,[4] sometimes have a foretaste.

Vain and brief is all human comfort.

Blessed and true is the comfort which is received inwardly from the truth.

A devout man everywhere carrieth with him his Comforter Jesus, and saith unto him, "Be thou present with me, O Lord Jesus, in every place and time.

"Let this be my consolation, to be cheerfully willing to do without all human comfort.

"And if thy consolation be wanting, let thy will and just trial of me be unto me as the greatest comfort; for thou wilt not always be angry, neither wilt thou threaten for ever."[5]

CHAPTER 17

That All Our Anxieties Are to Be Placed on God

My son, suffer Me to do with thee what I please. I know what is best for thee.

Thou thinkest as man; thou judgest in many things as human feelings persuade thee.

O Lord, what thou sayest is true. Thy anxiety

---

[4] Phil. 3:20   [5] Psalm 103:9

for me is greater[1] than all the care that I can take for myself.

For he standeth but very totteringly, who casteth not all his care upon thee.

O Lord, if only my will may remain right and firm toward thee, do with me whatever it shall please thee.

For it can not be anything but good, whatever thou shalt do with me.

2. If it be thy will I should be in darkness, be thou blessed; and if it be thy will I should be in light, be thou again blessed. If thou grant me comfort, be thou blessed; and if thou wilt have me afflicted, be thou still equally blessed.

My son, such as this ought to be thy state, if thou desire to walk with Me.

Thou must be as ready to suffer as to rejoice.

Thou must cheerfully be as destitute and poor, as full and rich.

3. O Lord, for thy sake, I will cheerfully suffer[2] whatever shall befall me with thy permission.

From thy hand I am willing to receive indifferently good and evil, sweet and bitter, joy and sorrow, and for all that befalleth me I will be thankful.

Keep me safe from all sin, and I shall fear neither death[3] nor hell.

---

[1]Matt. 6:30; John 6   [2]Job 2:10   [3]Psalm 23:4

So as thou dost not cast me from thee for ever, nor blot me out of the book of life, whatever tribulation may befall me shall not hurt me.

CHAPTER 18

That Temporal Miseries Must Be Borne Patiently, After the Example of Christ

My son, I descended from heaven[1] for thy salvation; I took upon Me thy miseries,[2] not necessity but charity drawing Me thereto; that thou thyself mightest learn patience, and bear temporal miseries without grudging.

For from the hour of my birth,[3] even until my death on the cross, I was not without suffering of grief.

I suffered great want of things temporal, I often heard many complaints against Me, I endured meekly disgraces and revilings; in return for benefits I received ingratitude, for miracles, blasphemies, for [heavenly] doctrine, reproofs.

2. O Lord, for that thou wert patient in thy lifetime, herein especially fulfilling the commandment of thy Father;[4] it is a reason that I, a most miserable sinner, should bear myself

---

[1]John 3:13   [2]Isaiah 53:4
[3]Luke 2:7   [4]John 5:30

patiently according to thy will, and for my soul's welfare endure the burden of this corruptible life as long as thou thyself shall choose for me.

For although this present life is burdensome, yet notwithstanding it is now by thy grace made very gainful; and by thy example and the footsteps of thy saints, more clear and endurable to the weak.

It is, too, much more full of consolation than it was, formerly in the old law, when the gate of heaven remained shut; and the way also to heaven seemed more obscure, when so few concerned themselves to seek after the kingdom of heaven.[5]

Moreover also they who then were just and such as should be saved, could not enter into the heavenly kingdom, before thy Passion, and the due payment of our debt by thy holy death.

3. Oh, what great thanks am I bound to render unto thee, that thou hast agreed to show unto me and to all faithful people the good and the right way to thine eternal kingdom.

For thy life is our way, and by holy patience we walk toward thee, who art our Crown.

If thou hadst not gone before us and taught us, who would have cared to follow!

Alas, how many would remain behind and afar off, if they considered not thy most noble example!

---

[5] Matt. 7:14

Behold, we are even yet cold, though we have heard of so many of thy miracles and doctrines; what would become of us, if we had not so great Light[6] whereby to follow thee!

CHAPTER 19

Of the Endurance of Injuries, and of the Proof of True Patience

What is it thou sayest, my son? Cease to complain, when thou considerest my Passion, and the sufferings of other holy persons.

Thou hast not yet resisted unto blood.[1]

It is but little which thou sufferest, in comparison with those who suffered so much, who were so strongly tempted, so grievously afflicted, so many ways tried and exercised.[2]

Thou oughtest therefore to call to mind the heavier sufferings of others, that so thou mayest the easier bear thy own very small troubles.

And if they seem unto thee not very small, then beware lest thy impatience be the cause thereof.

However, whether they be small or great, endeavor patiently to bear them all.

2. The better thou disposest thyself to suffering, so much the more wisely thou dost act, and so much the greater reward shalt thou receive;

---

[6]John 12:46   [1]Heb. 12:4   [2]Heb. 11:37

thou shalt also more easily endure it, if both in mind and by habit thou art diligently prepared thereunto.

Do not say, "I can not endure to suffer these things at the hands of such a man, nor are things of this sort to be suffered by me; for he hath done me great wrong, and charges me with things which I never thought of; but of another I will willingly suffer, things too which I shall see I ought to suffer."

Such a thought is foolish; it considereth not the virtue of patience, nor by whom it will be to be crowned; but rather weigheth too exactly the persons and the offenses committed.

3. He is not truly patient, who will only suffer so much as he thinks good, and from whom he pleases.

But the truly patient man minds not by whom he is exercised, whether by his superior, by one of his equals, or by an inferior; whether by a good and holy man; or by one that is perverse and unworthy.

But indifferently from every creature, how much soever, or how often soever anything adverse befalls him, he takes it all thankfully as from the hands of God, and esteems it a great gain.

For with God it is impossible that anything, however small, if only it be suffered for God's sake, should pass without its reward.

4. Be thou therefore [always] prepared for the fight, if thou wilt have the victory.

Without a combat thou canst not attain unto the crown of patience.[3]

If thou art unwilling to suffer, thou refusest to be crowned. But if thou desire to be crowned, fight manfully, endure patiently.

Without labor there is no coming to rest, nor without fighting can the victory be reached.

O Lord, let that become possible to me by thy grace, which by nature seems impossible to me.

Thou knowest that I am able to suffer but little, and that I am quickly cast down, when a slight adversity ariseth.

For thy name's sake, let every exercise of tribulation be made desirable to me; for to suffer and to be disquieted for thy sake, is very wholesome for my soul.

CHAPTER 20

Of the Acknowledging of Our Own Infirmities; and of the Miseries of This Life

I will confess against myself mine own unrighteousness;[1] I will confess my weakness unto Thee, O Lord.

Oftentimes a small matter it is that makes me sad and troubled.

I resolve that I will act with courage, but

---

[3] 2 Tim. 2:3-5   [1] Psalm 32:5

when even a small temptation comes, I am at once in great straits.

It is sometimes a very trifle, whence a great temptation arises.

And while I am thinking myself tolerably safe, and when I least expect it, I sometimes find myself almost entirely overcome with a slight breath.

2. Behold, therefore, O Lord, my low state;[2] and my frailty in every way known unto thee.

Have mercy on me, and deliver me out of the mire, that I may not stick fast therein,[3] may not remain utterly cast down for ever.

This it is which oftentimes drives me backward, and confounds me in thy sight, that I am so subject to fall, and weak in resisting my passions.

And although I do not altogether consent, yet their continual assaults are troublesome and grievous unto me; and it is exceedingly irksome to live thus daily in conflict.

Hence my weakness becomes known unto me, in that hateful fancies always much more easily rush into my mind than depart from it.

3. Most mighty God of Israel, thou zealous Lover of faithful souls! Oh, that thou wouldst consider the labor and sorrow of thy servant, and assist him in all things whatsoever he undertaketh.

Strengthen me with heavenly courage, lest

[2] Psalm 25:18   [3] Psalm 69:14

the old man, the miserable flesh, not as yet fully subject to the spirit, prevail and get the upper hand; against which it will be needful for me to fight, as long as I breathe in this miserable life.

Alas, what kind of life is this, where tribulation and miseries are never wanting; where all is full of snares, and enemies!

For when one tribulation or temptation retreateth, another cometh on; yea, and while the first conflict continues, many others come unexpected one after another.

4. And how can a life be loved that hath so great bitterness, and is subject to so many calamities and miseries?

Again, how is it called life, that generates so many deaths and plagues?

And yet it is the object of men's love, and many seek to delight themselves therein.

The world is oftentimes blamed for being deceitful and vain, and yet men do not easily part with it, because the desires of the flesh bear so great a sway.

But some things draw us to love the world, others to despise it.

The lust of the flesh, the lust of the eyes, and the pride of life,[4] do draw us to the love of the world; but the pains and miseries that do justly follow these things cause a hatred of the world and a loathsomeness thereof.

5. But, alas, the fondness for evil pleasures

---

[4] 1 John 2:16

overcometh the mind of him who is addicted to the world; and he esteemeth it a delight to be under thorns,[5] because he hath not seen or tasted the sweetness of God, and the inward pleasantness of virtue.

But they who perfectly despise the world, and study to live to God under holy discipline, these are not ignorant of the divine sweetness promised to those who truly forsake the world; they also very clearly see how grievously the world is mistaken, and how it is in many ways deceived.

CHAPTER 21

That We Are to Rest in God Above All Things Which Are Good, and Above All His Own Gifts

Above all things, and in all things, O my soul, thou shalt rest in the Lord always, for he himself is the everlasting rest of the saints.

Grant me, O most sweet and loving Jesus, to rest in thee above all creatures,[1] above all health and beauty, above all glory and honor, above all power and dignity, above all knowledge and subtilty, above all riches and arts, above all joy and gladness, above all fame and praise, above all sweetness and comfort, above all hope and promise, above all desert and desire:

---

[5] Job 30:7   [1] Rom. 8:19-22

Above all gifts and presents that thou canst give and impart unto us, above all mirth and jubilation that the mind of man can receive and feel:

Finally, above angels and archangels, and above all the heavenly host, above all visible and invisible things, and above all that thou art not, O my God.

2. Because thou, O Lord, my God, art supremely good above all; thou alone art most high, thou alone most powerful, thou alone most full and sufficient, thou alone most sweet and most full of consolation.

Thou alone art most beautiful and loving, thou alone most noble and glorious above all things, in whom all good things together both perfectly are, and ever have been, and shall be.

And therefore it is too small, and unsatisfying, whatever thou bestowest on me beside thyself, or revealest unto me of thyself, or dost promise, while thou art not seen, and not fully obtained.

For surely my heart can not truly rest, nor be entirely contented, unless it rest in thee, and transcend all gifts and all creatures whatsoever.

3. O thou most beloved spouse of my soul, Jesus Christ, thou most pure Lover, thou Lord of all creation: Oh, that I had the wings of true liberty, that I might fly away and rest in thee![2]

---

[2] Psalm 55:6

Oh, when shall it be fully granted to me, to consider in quietness of mind and see how sweet thou art, my Lord God!

When shall I fully collect myself in thee, that by reason of my love to thee I may not feel myself, but thee alone, above all sense and measure, in a manner not known to all![3]

But now I oftentimes sigh, and bear my unhappiness with grief.

Because many evils occur in this vale of miseries, which do often trouble, grieve, and cover me with a cloud; often hinder and distract me, allure, and entangle me, so that I can have no free access unto thee, nor enjoy the sweet welcomings, which are ever ready for the blessed spirits.

Oh, let my sighs move thee, and my manifold desolation here on earth.

4. O Jesus, thou brightness of eternal glory, thou comfort of the pilgrim-soul, with thee is my mouth without voice, and my very silence speaketh unto thee.

How long doth my Lord delay to come?

Let him come unto me, his poor despised servant, and let him make me glad. Let him put forth his hand, and deliver a poor wretch from all anguish.

Come, oh, come; for without thee I shall have no joyful day nor hour; for thou art my joy, and without thee my table is empty.

---

[3]Dan. 10

A wretched creature I am, and in a manner imprisoned and loaded with fetters, until thou refresh me with the light of thy presence, and grant me liberty, and show a friendly countenance toward me.

5. Let others seek what they please instead of thee; but for me, nothing else doth nor shall delight me, but thou only, my God, my hope, my everlasting salvation.

I will not hold my peace, nor cease to pray, until thy grace return again, and thou speak inwardly unto me.

Behold, here I am. Behold, I come unto thee, because thou hast called upon Me. Thy tears and the desire of thy soul, thy humiliation and thy contrition of heart, have inclined and brought me unto thee.

And I said, Lord, I have called thee, and have desired to enjoy thee, being ready to refuse all things for thee.

For thou first hast stirred me up, that I might seek thee.

Blessed be thou therefore, O Lord, that has showed this goodness to thy servant, according to the multitude of thy mercies.

6. What hath thy servant more to say before thee? He can only greatly humble himself in they sight, ever mindful of his own iniquity and vileness.

For there is none like unto thee[4] in all whatever is wonderful in heaven and earth.

Thy works are very good, thy judgments true, and by thy providence the universe is governed.

Praise therefore, and glory be unto thee, O Wisdom of the Father: let my mouth, my soul, and all creatures together, praise and bless thee.

CHAPTER 22

Of the Remembrance of God's Manifold Benefits

Open, O Lord, my heart in thy law, and teach me to walk in thy commandments.[1]

Grant me to understand thy will, and with great reverence and diligent consideration to remember thy benefits, as well in general as in particular, that henceforward I may be able worthily to give thee thanks.

But I know, and confess, that I am not able, even in the least point, to give thee due thanks for the favors which thou bestowest upon me.

I am less than the least of all thy benefits: and when I consider thy noble bounty, the greatness thereof maketh my spirit to faint.

2. All that we have in our soul and body, and whatsoever we possess outwardly or inward-

---

[4]Psalm 35:8   [1]Psalm 119

ly, naturally or supernaturally, are thy benefits, and do speak thee bountiful, merciful, and good, from whom we have received all good things.

Although one have received more, another less, all notwithstanding are thine, and without thee even the least blessing can not be had.

He that hath received greater can not glory of his own merit, nor extol himself above others, nor insult the lesser: for he is the greater and the better who ascribeth least unto himself, and is the most humble and devout in rendering thanks.

And he that esteemeth himself the vilest of all men, and judgeth himself most unworthy, is fittest to receive the greater blessings.

3. But he that hath received fewer, ought not to be saddened, nor take it grievously, nor envy them that are enriched with greater store; but rather turn his mind to thee, and highly praise thy goodness, for that thou bestowest thy gifts so bountifully, so freely, and so willingly, without respect of persons.

All things proceed from thee, and therefore in all things thou art to be praised.

Thou knowest what is fit to be given to every one; and why this man hath less and that more, it is not for us to judge, but for thee who dost exactly know what is appropriate for every one.

4. Wherefore, O Lord God, I even esteem it a great mercy, not to have much of that which outwardly and in the opinion of men seems

worthy of glory and applause. For so it is, that he who considers the poverty and unworthiness of his person, should not therefore conceive grief or sadness, or be cast down thereat, but rather should take great comfort, and be glad; because thou, O God, hast chosen the poor, and humble, and the despised of this world for thyself,[2] and for thy familiar and domestic attendants.

Witnesses are thy Apostles themselves, whom thou hast made princes over all the earth.[3]

And yet they lived in the world without complaint,[4] so humble and simple, without all malice and deceit, that they even rejoiced to suffer reproach for thy name;[5] and what the world despises, they embraced with great affection.

5. When therefore a man loveth thee and acknowledgeth thy benefits, nothing ought so to rejoice him as thy will toward him, and the good pleasure of thy eternal appointment.

And herewith he ought to be so contented and comforted, that he would as willingly be the least, as another would wish to be the greatest.

He would too be as peaceable and contented in the last place as in the first; as willing to be a despised cast-away, of no name or character, as

---

[2] 1 Cor. 1:27   [3] Psalm 45:16
[4] 1 Thess. 2:10   [5] Acts 5:41

to be preferred in honor before others, and to be greater in the world than they.

For thy will and the love of thy glory ought to be preferred before all things, and to comfort him more, and please him better, than all the benefits which either he hath received or may receive

CHAPTER 23

Of Four Things That Bring Much Inward Peace

My son, now I will teach thee the way of peace and true liberty.

O Lord, I beseech thee, do as thou sayest, for this is a great joy to me to hear

Endeavor, my son, rather to do the will of another than thine own.[1]
Choose always to have less rather than more.[2]
Seek always the lowest place, and to be inferior to every one.[3]
Wish always, and pray, that the will of God may be wholly fulfilled in thee.[4]
Behold, such a man entereth within the borders of peace and rest.

---

[1]Matt. 26:39; John 5:30; 6:38   [2]1 Cor. 10:24
[3]Luke 14:10   [4]Matt. 6:10

2. O Lord, this thy short speech containeth within itself much perfection.[5]

It is little in words, but full in meaning, and abundant in fruit.

For if I could faithfully observe it, I ought not to be so easily troubled.

For as often as I feel myself unquiet and disturbed, I find that I have strayed from this doctrine.

But thou who canst do all things, and ever lovest the profiting of my soul, increase in me thy grace, that I may fulfil thy works, and work out mine own salvation.

3. *A prayer against evil thoughts*

O Lord my God, be not thou far from me; my God, have regard to help me;[6] for various evil thoughts have risen up against me, and great fears, afflicting my soul.

How shall I pass through them without hurt? How shall I utterly break them?

"I will go before thee," saith he, "and will humble the great ones of the earth; I will open the doors of the prison, and reveal unto thee hidden secrets."[7]

Do, O Lord, as thou sayest, and let all my evil thoughts fly from before thy face.

This is my hope, my only consolation, to flee unto thee in every tribulation, to trust in thee,

---

[5]Matt. 5:48   [6]Psalm 71:12   [7]Isaiah 14:2-3

to call upon thee from my heart, and to wait patiently for thy consolation.

4. A *prayer for mental illumination*

O merciful Jesus, enlighten thou me with a clear shining inward light, and drive away all darkness from dwelling in my heart.

Repress thou my many wandering thoughts, and destroy those temptations which violently assault me.

Fight thou strongly for me, and vanquish the evil beasts, I mean the alluring desires of the flesh, that so peace may be obtained by thy power, and that thine abundant praise may resound in thy holy court, that is, in a pure conscience.

Command the winds and storms; say unto the sea, Be still,[8] and to the north wind, Blow not, and there shall be a great calm.

5. Send out thy light and thy truth,[9] that they may shine upon the earth; for until thou enlighten me, I am but as earth, without form and void.

Pour forth thy grace from above, fill my heart with heavenly dew, supply fresh streams of devotion, to water the face of the earth, that it may bring forth fruit good and excellent.

Lift thou up my mind which is pressed down by a load of sins, and draw up my whole desire to things heavenly; that having tasted the

---

[8]Matt. 8:26   [9]Psalm 43:3

sweetness of divine happiness, it may be irksome to me even to think about earthly things.

6. Do thou pluck me away, and deliver me from all transitory consolation of creatures; for no created thing can give full comfort and rest to my desires.

Join thou me to thyself with an inseparable band of love; for thou even alone dost satisfy him that loveth thee, and without thee all things are vain and frivolous.

CHAPTER 24

Of Avoiding Curious Inquiry
Into Other Men's Lives

My son, be not curious, nor trouble thyself with idle cares.[1]

What is this or that to thee? follow thou Me.[2]

For what is it to thee, whether that man be such or such, or whether this man do or speak this or that?

Thou shalt not need to answer for others, but shalt give account for thyself;[3] why therefore dost thou entangle thyself?

Behold, I know every one, and do see all things that are done under the sun; also I understand how it is with every one, what he

---

[1] Ecclus. 3:23; 1 Tim. 5:13
[2] John 21:22   [3] Gal. 6:4-5

thinks, what he wishes, and at what his intentions aim.

Unto Me therefore all things are to be committed; but do thou keep thyself gently at peace, and let go the unquiet, to be as unquiet as they will.

Whatsoever they shall have done or said, shall come upon themselves, for Me they can not deceive.

2. Be not solicitous for the shadow of a great name, or for the familiar friendship of many, or for the private affection of individuals.

For these things both distract the heart, and greatly darken it.

Gladly would I speak my word, and reveal my secrets unto thee, if thou wouldest diligently observe my coming, and open unto Me the door of thy heart.

Be thou careful, and watchful in prayer, and in all things humble thyself.

CHAPTER 25

Wherein Firm Peace of Heart and True Spiritual Progress Consisteth

My son, I have said, "Peace I leave with you, my peace I give unto you: not as the world giveth, give I unto you."[1]

---

[1] John 14:27

Peace is what all desire, but all do not care for the things that pertain unto true peace.

My peace is with the humble and gentle of heart; in much patience shall thy peace be.

If thou wilt hear Me and follow my voice, thou shalt be able to enjoy much peace.

What then shall I do, O Lord?

In every matter attend to thyself, what thou doest, and what thou sayest; and direct thy whole attention unto this, that thou mayest please me alone, and neither desire nor seek anything beside me.

But as for the words or deeds of others judge nothing rashly; neither do thou entangle thyself with things not committed unto thee; and doing thus thou mayest be little or seldom disturbed.

2. But never to feel any grief at all, nor to suffer any trouble of mind or body, belongs not to this life, but to the state of eternal rest.

Think not therefore that thou hast found true peace, if thou feel no burden; nor that then all is well, if thou have no adversary; nor that "to be perfect," is to have all things done according to thy desire.

Neither do thou then esteem highly of thyself, or account thyself to be specially beloved, if thou be in a state of great devotion and sweetness; for it is not by these things that a true lover of virtue is known, nor doth the progress and perfection of a man consist in these things.

3. In what then, O Lord? In giving thyself over with all thy heart to the divine will, not seeking thine own interest, either in great matters or in small, either in time or in eternity.

And so thou shalt keep one and the same countenance, with thanksgiving, both in prosperity and in adversity, weighing all things with an equal balance.

Be thou of such courage, and so patient in hope, that when inward comfort is withdrawn, thou mayest prepare thy heart to suffer even greater things; and do not justify thyself, as though thou ought not to suffer these afflictions, or any so great, but acknowledge me in whatsoever I appoint, and still praise my holy name.

Then shalt thou walk in the true and right way of and thou shalt have undoubted hope to see my face again with great delight.

For if thou attain to the entire contempt of thyself, know that thou shalt then enjoy abundance of peace, as great as this thy state of sojourning is capable of.

CHAPTER 26

Of the Excellence of a Free Mind, Which Is Sooner Gained By Humble Prayer Than By Reading

O Lord, it is the work of a perfect man, never to relax his mind from attentive thought of heavenly things, and so to pass amid many cares, as it were, without care; not as one destitute of all feeling, but by the prerogative of a free mind, adhering to no creature with inordinate affection.

2. I beseech thee, my most gracious God, preserve me from the cares of this life, lest I should be too much entangled by them; also from the many necessities of the body, lest I should be captivated by pleasure; and from whatever is an obstacle to the soul, lest being broken with troubles, I should be overthrown.

I speak not of those things which worldly vanity so earnestly covets, but of those miseries, which as punishments, and as the common curse of mortality,[1] do weigh down and hinder the soul of thy servant, that it can not enter into the freedom of the spirit so often as it would.

3. O my God, thou sweetness ineffable, make bitter for me all carnal comfort, which

---

[1]Gen. 3:17; Rom. 7:11

draws me away from the love of eternal things, and in evil manner allures me to itself by setting before me some present delightful good.

Let me not be overcome, O Lord, let me not be overcome by flesh and blood;[2] let not the world and the short glory thereof deceive me; let not the devil and his subtle craftiness supplant me.

Give me strength to resist, patience to endure, and constancy to persevere.

Give me, instead of all the comforts of the world, the most sweet balm of thy Spirit, and instead of carnal love, influence with the love of thy name.

4. Behold! meat, drink, clothes, and other necessaries for the maintenance of the body, are burdensome unto a fervent spirit.

Grant me to use such refreshments moderately, and not to be entangled with an over-great desire for them.

It is not lawful to cast away all things, because nature is to be sustained; but to desire superfluities, and those things that are merely for delight, the holy law forbiddeth us; for then the flesh would rebel against the spirit. Herein, I beseech thee, let thy hand govern me and teach me, that I may not exceed the due bounds.

---

[2]Rom. 12:21

CHAPTER 27

That It Is Self-Love Which Most Hindereth
From the Chiefest Good

My son, thou must give all for all, and retain nothing of thyself.

Know, that the love of thyself doth hurt thee more than anything in the world.

According to the love and affection thou bearest them, so doth everything cleave unto thee more or less.

If thy love be pure,[1] simple, and well-ordered, thou shalt be free from the bondage of things.

Do not covet that which it is not lawful for thee to have. Do not covet that which may hinder thee, and deprive thee of inward liberty.

Strange it is that thou committest not thyself wholly unto Me, from the bottom of thy heart, with all things thou canst have or desire.

2. Why dost thou pine away with vain grief?[2] why tire thyself with needless cares?

Accept my good pleasure, and thou shalt suffer no detriment at all.

If thou seek this or that, and wouldest be here or there, the better to enjoy thine own profit and pleasure, thou shalt never be at rest, nor free from trouble of mind; for in every instance

---

[1] Matt. 6:22   [2] Exodus 18:18; Mic. 4:9

something will be wanting, and in every place there will be some one to cross thee.

Our welfare then lies not in obtaining and heaping together any external things, but rather in despising them, and utterly rooting them out from the heart.

And this thou must understand not of income and wealth only, but of seeking after honor also, and the desire of empty praise, all which do pass away with this world.

The place availeth little if the spirit of fervor be wanting, neither shall that peace long continue, which is sought from without;[3] if the state of thy heart be destitute of a true foundation, that is, unless thou stand steadfast in Me, thou mayest change but not better thyself.

For when occasion arises, and is laid hold of, thou shalt find what thou didst fly from, and more too.

4. *A prayer for a clean heart, and heavenly wisdom*

Strengthen me, O God, by the grace of thy Holy Spirit.[4]

Grant me to be strengthened with might in the inner man,[5] and to cast out of my heart all useless care and anguish;[6] not to be drawn away with various desires of anything, whether vile or precious, but to look upon all things as passing

---

[3]Isaiah 41:13 [4]Psalm 2:12
[5]Eph. 3:16 [6]Matt. 6:34

away, and on myself also as passing away together with them.

For nothing is permanent under the sun, where all things are vanity and vexation of spirit.[7] Oh, how wise is he that so considereth them!

5. O Lord, grant me heavenly wisdom,[8] that I may learn above all things to seek and to find thee, above all things to relish and to love thee, and to understand all other things as they are, according to the order of thy wisdom.

Grant that I may prudently avoid him that flatters me, and suffer patiently him that contradicts me.

For it is a great part of wisdom not to be moved with every blast of words,[9] nor to give ear to an ill, flattering siren; for thus we shall go on securely in the way we have begun.

CHAPTER 28

Against the Tongues of Slanderers

My son, take it not to heart if some think ill of thee,[1] and speak that which thou wouldest not willingly hear.

---

[7]Eccles. 1:14; 2:1   [8]Wisd. 9:4
[9]Eph. 4:14   [1]1 Cor. 4:13

Thou oughtest to judge the worst of thyself, and to think no man weaker than thyself.

If thou dost walk spiritually, thou wilt not much weigh fleeting words.

It is no small wisdom to keep silence in an evil time, and inwardly to turn thyself to Me, nor to be troubled by the judgment of men.

2. Let not thy peace depend on the tongues of men; for whether they speak well or ill, thou art not therefore another man. Where are true peace and true glory? Are they not in Me?[2]

And he that desireth not to please men, nor feareth to displease them, shall enjoy much peace.

From inordinate love and vain fear ariseth all disquiet of heart and distraction of mind.

CHAPTER 29

How We Ought to Call Upon God, and to Bless Him, When Tribulation Is Upon Us

Blessed, O Lord, be thy name for ever;[1] for that it pleaseth thee that this temptation and tribulation should come upon me.

I can not escape it, but must needs flee to thee, that thou mayest help me, and turn it to my good.

Lord, I am now in affliction, and it is not well

---

[2]John 16:33   [1]Job 1:21; Psalm 113:2

with my mind, but I am much troubled with my present suffering.

And now, dear Father, what shall I say?[2] I am caught amid adversities; save thou me from this hour.

Yet therefore came I unto this hour, that thou mayest be glorified, when I shall be greatly humbled, and by thee delivered.

Let it please thee, Lord, to deliver me;[3] for poor wretch that I am, what can I do, and whither shall I go without thee?

Grant me patience, O Lord, even now in this emergency. Help me, my God, and then I will not fear how deeply I may be afflicted.

2. And now in these my troubles what shall I say?

Lord, thy will be done;[4] I have well deserved to be afflicted and grieved.

Surely I ought to bear it; and oh that I may bear it with patience, until the tempest passes over, and it becomes calm!

But thy omnipotent hand is able to take even this temptation from me, and to moderate its violence thereof, that I utterly sink not under it; as oftentimes heretofore thou hast done unto me, O my God, my Mercy!

And the more difficult it is to me, so much the easier to thee is this change of the right-hand of the Most High.

---

[2] Matt. 26 [or John 12:27]
[3] Psalm 37:40   [4] Matt. 6:10

CHAPTER 30

Of Craving the Divine Aid, and Confidence of
Recovering Grace

My son, I am the Lord that giveth strength in the day of tribulation.[1]

Come thou unto me, when it is not well with thee.[2]

This is that which most of all hindereth heavenly comfort, that thou art too slow in turning thyself unto prayer.

For before thou dost earnestly supplicate me, thou seekest in the meanwhile many comforts, and delightest thyself in outward things.

And hence it comes to pass that all doth little profit thee, until thou consider well that I am he who delivereth them that trust in me; and that out of me, there is neither powerful help, nor profitable counsel, nor lasting remedy.

But do thou, having now recovered breath after the tempest, gather strength again in the light of my mercies; for I am at hand, saith the Lord, to repair all, not only entirely, but also abundantly and in most plentiful measure.

2. Is there anything difficult to me? Or am I like unto one that promiseth and performeth not?[3]

Where is thy faith? Stand firmly and with

---

[1]Nahum 1:7   [2]Matt. 11:28   [3]Matt. 23:35

perseverance; take courage and be patient; comfort will come to thee in due time.

Wait, wait, for me: I will come and heal thee.

It is a temptation that vexeth thee, and a vain fear that troubles thee.

What else doth anxiety about future contingencies bring thee, but sorrow upon sorrow? "Sufficient for the day is the evil thereof."[4]

It is a vain thing and unprofitable, to be either disturbed or pleased about future things, which perhaps will never come to pass.

3. But it is in the nature of man to be deluded with such imaginations; and a sign of a mind as yet weak, to be so easily drawn away by the suggestion of the enemy.

For so he may delude and deceive thee, he careth not whether it be by true or by false propositions; whether he overthrow thee with the love of present, or the fear of future things.

Let not therefore thy heart be troubled, neither let it be afraid.

Trust in me, and put thy confidence in my mercy.[5]

When thou thinkest thyself farthest from me, oftentimes I am nearest unto thee.

When thou judgest that almost all is lost, then oftentimes the greatest gain of reward is close at hand.

All is not lost, when anything falleth out contrary.

---

[4]Matt. 6:34   [5]Psalm 91:1

Thou must not judge according to present feeling; nor so take any grief, or give thyself up to it, from wherever it cometh, as though all hopes of recovery were quite gone.

4. Think not thyself wholly forsaken, although for a time I have sent thee some tribulation, or withdrawn thy desired comfort; for this is the way to the kingdom of heaven.

And without doubt it is more expedient for thee and the rest of my servants, that ye be exercised in adversities, than that ye should have all things according to your inclinations.

I know the hidden thoughts of thy heart, and that it is very expedient for thy welfare, that thou be left sometimes without taste of spiritual sweetness, and in a dry condition, lest perhaps thou shouldest be vain about thy prosperous estate, and shouldest be willing to please thyself in that which thou art not.

That which I have given, I can take away; and restore it again when I please.

5. When I give it, it is still mine; when I withdraw it again, I take not anything that is thine; for mine is every good and every perfect gift.[6]

If I send thee affliction, or any cross whatsoever, do not be saddened, nor let thy heart fail thee; I can quickly succor thee, and turn all thy heaviness into joy.

---

[6]James 1:17

However I am righteous, and greatly to be praised when I deal thus with thee.

6. If thou be wise, and considerest this rightly, thou wilt never mourn so dejectedly for any adversity that befalleth thee, but rather rejoice and give thanks.

Yea, thou wilt account this thy special joy, that afflicting thee with sorrows, I do not spare thee.

"As my Father hath loved me, I also love you,"[7] said I unto my beloved disciples; whom certainly I sent not out to temporal joys, but to great conflicts; not to honors, but to contempts; not to idleness, but to labors; not to rest, but to bring forth much fruit with patience. Remember thou these words, O my son!

CHAPTER 31

Of the Contempt of All Creatures, to Find Out the Creator

O Lord, I stand much in need of yet greater grace, if I ought to reach that pitch, where neither man nor any creature shall be a hinderance unto me.

For as long as anything detains me, I can not freely take my flight to thee.

---

[7] John 15:9

He desired to fly freely to thee that said, "Who will give me wings like a dove, and I will flee away and be at rest?"[1]

What thing can be more quiet than the single eye?[2] and what more free, than he that desireth nothing upon earth?

A man ought therefore to rise above all creatures, and perfectly to forsake himself and stand in ecstasy of mind, and see that thou, the Creator of all things, hast nothing amongst creatures like unto thyself.

Unless a person be disengaged from all creatures, he can not with freedom of mind attend unto divine things.

For that is the cause why there are so few contemplative persons to be found, for that few can wholly withdraw themselves from things created and perishing.

2. To obtain this there is need of much grace, such as may elevate the soul, and carry it away above itself.

And unless a man be elevated in spirit, and freed from all creatures, and wholly united unto God, whatever he knoweth, and whatever he hath, is of no great importance.

For a long while shall he be small, and lie groveling below, whoever he is that esteemeth anything great, but the One only Infinite Eternal God.

---

[1]Psalm 55:6   [2]Matt. 6:22

And whatever is not God, is nothing, and ought to be accounted as nothing.

There is great difference between the wisdom of an illuminated and devout man, and the knowledge of a learned and studious cleric.

Far more noble is that learning which floweth from above, from the Divine Influence, than that which is painfully gotten by the learning of man.

3. There are many that desire contemplation, but they endeavor not to practise those things that are required to attain it.

A great hinderance it is, that men rest in signs and sensible things, and take little care about the perfect abasement of themselves.

I know not what it is, by what spirit we are led, nor what we pretend, we that seem to be called spiritual, that we take so much pains, and are so full of anxiety about transitory and low things, and scarcely even seldom think of our own inward concerns, with full recollection of mind.

4. Alas, presently after a slight recollection, we break out again, and weigh not our works with strict examination.

We mind not where our affections lie, nor lament the impurity that is in all our actions.

For "all flesh had corrupted his way," and therefore did the great deluge follow.[3]

----

[3] Gen. 6:12; 7:21

Since then our inward affection is much corrupted, our actions thence proceeding must needs be corrupted also, proofs of the lack of inward vigor.

From a pure heart proceedeth the fruit of a good life.

5. We ask how much a man has done, but from what degree of virtuous principle he acts, is not so studiously considered.

We inquire whether he be courageous, rich, handsome, skilful, a good writer, a good singer, or a good laborer; but how poor he is in spirit, how patient and meek, how devout and spiritual, is seldom spoken of.

Nature looks upon the outward things of a man, grace turneth itself to the inward.

The one is often disappointed; the other hath her trust in God, and so is not deceived.

CHAPTER 32

Of Self-Denial, and Renouncing Every Evil Appetite

My son, thou canst not possess perfect liberty unless thou wholly deny thyself.[1]

They are but in fetters all who merely seek their own interest, and are lovers of themselves;

---

[1] Matt. 16:24; 19:8-9

covetous are they, curious, wanderers, always seeking delicates, not the things of Jesus Christ, but oftentimes devising and framing that which will not stand.

For all that is not of God shall perish.

Keep this short and perfect word: "Forsake all, and thou shalt find all." Leave all inordinate desire and thou shalt find rest.

Consider this well, and when thou hast put it into practice, thou shalt understand all things.

O Lord, this is not the work of one day, nor children's sport; yea, rather in this short sentence is included all the perfection of religious persons.

2. My son, thou oughtest not to turn back, nor at once to be cast down, when thou hearest of the way of the perfect; but rather be stirred up to higher things, or at least in desire sigh after them.

I would it were so with thee, and thou wert come so far, to be no longer a lover of thyself, but didst stand merely at my bidding, and at his whom I have appointed a father over thee, then thou shouldest exceedingly please Me, and all thy life would pass away in joy and peace.

Thou hast yet many things to part with, which, unless thou wholly give them up to Me, thou shalt not attain to that which thou desirest.

"I counsel thee to buy of Me gold tried in the

fire, that thou mayest become rich;"[2] that is, heavenly wisdom, which treadeth under-foot all inferior and earthly things.

Set little by earthly wisdom, and care not fondly to please others or thyself.

3. I said that lowly things must be bought with things which, among men, are precious and of great esteem.

For true heavenly wisdom doth seem ordinary, of small account, and almost forgotten among men, as having no high thoughts of itself, nor seeking to be magnified upon earth. Many indeed praise it with their mouth, but in their life they are far from it; yet is it the precious pearl,[3] which is hidden from many.

CHAPTER 33

Of Inconstancy of Heart, and of Having Our Final Intentions Directed Unto God

My son, trust not to thy feeling, for it will quickly be changed into something else.

As long as thou livest, thou art subject to change,[1] even against thy will; so that thou art at one time merry, then sad; at one time quiet,

---

[2]Rev. 3:18   [3]Matt. 13:46   [1]Job 14:2

then troubled; now devout, then worldly; now diligent, then listless; now grave, and presently light-hearted.

But he that is wise and well instructed in the spirit standeth firm upon these changeable things; not heeding what he feeleth in himself, or which way the wind of instability bloweth; but that the whole intention of his mind may tend to the right and best end.

For thus he will be able to continue one and the self-same, and unshaken, in the midst of so many various events directing continually the single eye of his intention unto Me.

2. And the purer the eye of the intention is,[2] with so much the more constancy doth a man pass through the several kinds of storms which assail him.

But in many the eye of a pure intention grows dim, for it quickly looks upon some pleasureable object which comes in its way.

For it is rare to find one who is wholly free from all blemish of self-seeking.

So the Jews formerly came to Bethany to Martha and Mary, not for Jesus's sake only, but that they might see Lazarus also.[3]

The eye of our intention therefore is to be purified, that it may be single and right,[4] and is to be directed unto me, beyond all the various circumstances which may come between.

---

[2]Matt. 6:22   [3]John 12:9   [4]Matt. 6:22

CHAPTER 34

That God Is Sweet Above All Things, and in All Things, to Him That Loveth Him

"Behold! my God, and all things [to me]."
What would I more, and what greater happiness can I desire?

O sweet and savory word! but to him only that loveth the word, not the world nor those things that are in the world.

"My God, and my all!" Enough is said to him that understandeth; and to him that loveth, it is pleasant to repeat it often.

For when thou art present, all things do yield delight, but when thou art absent, everything becomes irksome.

Thou givest quietness of heart, and much peace, and festive joy.

Thou makest us to think well of all things, and praise thee in all things; neither can anything become lasting pleasure without thee: but if it be pleasant and grateful, thy grace must be present, and it must be seasoned with the sweetness of thy wisdom.

2. What is not delightful unto him to whom thou art pleasing.

And whom thou delightest not, what can be pleasant to him?

But the wise men of the world, and they also who relish the things of the flesh, come short of thy wisdom,[1] for in the one is much vanity, and in the other death.

But they that follow thee by the contempt of worldly things, and mortification of the flesh, are found to be truly wise; for they are changed from vanity to truth, from the flesh to the spirit.

These relish God; and whatever good is found in creatures, they wholly refer unto the praise of their Maker.

Great, however, yea, very great is the difference between the sweetness of the Creator, and of the creature, of Eternity and of time, of Light uncreated and of light enlightened.

3. O thou Everlasting Light, surpassing all created lights, dart the beams of thy brightness from above which may pierce all the most inward recesses of my heart.

Purify, rejoice, enlighten and enliven my spirit, with all the powers thereof, that I may cleave unto thee with abundance of joy and triumph.

Oh, when will that blessed and desired hour come, that thou mayest fill me with thy presence, and thou mayest be unto me all in all.

As long as this is not granted me, I shall not have full joy.

Still, alas! the old Man doth live in me,[2] he is not wholly crucified, is not perfectly dead.

---

[1] 1 Cor. 1:26; Rom. 8:5; 1 John 2:16   [2] Rom. 7

Still doth he mightily strive against the Spirit, and stirreth up inward wars, and suffereth not the kingdom of my soul to be in peace.

4. But thou that rulest the power of the sea, and stillest the rising of the waves thereof,[3] arise and help me!

Scatter the nations that desire war,[4] crush thou them by thy might.

Display thy greatness, I beseech thee and let thy right hand be glorified, for there is no other hope or refuge for me, save in thee, O Lord my God.[5]

CHAPTER 35

*That There Is No Security From Temptation
in This Life*

My son, thou art never secure in this life, but as long as thou livest,[1] thou shalt always need spiritual armor.

Thou dwellest among enemies, and art assaulted on the right hand and on the left.[2]

If therefore thou defend not thyself on every side with the shield of patience, thou wilt not be long without a wound.

---

[3]Psalm 89:9   [4]Psalm 68:30   [5]Psalm 31:14
[1]Job 7:1   [2]2 Cor. 6:7

Moreover, if thou fix not thy heart on Me with a sincere willingness to suffer all things for Me, thou canst not bear the heat of this combat, nor attain to the palm of the saints in bliss.

Thou oughtest therefore manfully to go through all, and to secure a strong hand against whatever withstandeth thee.

For to him that overcometh is manna given, but for the indolent there remains much misery.

2. If thou seek rest in this world, how wilt thou then attain to the everlasting rest?

Dispose not thyself for much rest, but for much patience.

Seek true peace not in earth, but in heaven; not in men, nor in any other creature, but in God alone.

For the love of God thou oughtest cheerfully to undergo all things, that is to say, all labor, grief, temptation, vexation, anxiety, necessity, infirmity, injury, detraction, reproof, humiliation, shame, correction, and contempt.

These help to virtue; these are the trial of a novice in Christ; these frame the heavenly crown.

I will give an everlasting reward for a short labor, and infinite glory for transitory shame.

3. Thinkest thou that thou shalt always have spiritual consolations at will?

My saints had not so, but they had many afflictions, and sundry temptations, and great discomforts.

But in all these they did bear themselves up patiently, and trusted rather in God than in themselves, knowing that the sufferings of this time are not worthy to be compared to future glory.[3]

Wilt thou have that at once, which others, after many tears and great labors, have hardly obtained?

Wait for the Lord, behave thyself manfully, and be of good courage;[4] do not despair, do not leave thy place, but steadily offer both body and soul for the glory of God.

I will reward thee in most plentiful manner; I will be with thee in every tribulation.

CHAPTER 36

Against the Vain Judgments of Men

My son, cast thy heart firmly on the Lord, and fear not the judgment of men, when conscience gives testimony of thy piety and innocency.

It is a good and happy thing to suffer in such a way; nor will it be burdensome to a heart which is humble, and which trusteth rather in God than in itself.

---

[3]Rom. 8:18   [4]Psalm 27:14

The most part of men are given to talk much, and therefore little trust is to be placed in them.

Moreover also, to satisfy all is not possible.

Although Paul endeavored to please all in the Lord, and made himself all things unto all,[1] yet with him it was a very small thing that he should be judged of man's judgment.[2]

He did for the edification and salvation of others whatever lay in him, and as much as he was able; yet could he not prevent it that he was sometimes judged and despised by others.

Therefore he committed all to God, who knew all, and he defended himself with patience and humility against unjust tongues, or against those who thought vanities and lies, and spake boastfully whatever they desired.

Sometimes notwithstanding he made answer, lest the weak should be offended by his silence.[3]

3. Who art thou that fearest a mortal man? Today he is, and to-morrow he is no more seen.[4]

Fear God, and thou shalt not need to fear the terrors of men.

What harm can the words or injuries of any man do thee? He hurteth himself rather than thee, nor can he avoid the judgment of God[5] whoever he may be.

---

[1] 1 Cor. 9:22; 2 Cor. 4:2   [2] Col. 1; 1 Cor. 4:3
[3] Acts 26; Phil. 1:14   [4] 1 Mac. 2:62-63
[5] Rom. 2:3; 1 Cor. 11:32

Have thou God before thine eyes, and contend not with complaining words.

And if for the present thou seem to be overcome, and to suffer shame undeservedly, do not therefore repine, neither do thou lessen thy crown by thy impatience.[6]

But rather lift thou up thine eyes to Me in heaven, who am able to deliver thee from all shame and wrong, and to render to every man according to his works.

CHAPTER 37

*Of Pure and Entire Resignation of Ourselves,
For the Obtaining Freedom of Heart*

My son, forsake thyself, and thou shalt find Me.[1]

Make no self-respecting choice of anything, nor appropriate anything to thyself, and thou shalt ever be a gainer.

For greater grace shall be added to thee, the moment thou dost perfectly resign thyself, if thou dost not turn back to take thyself again.

Lord, how often shall I resign myself, and wherein shall I forsake myself?

---

[6]Heb. 12:1-2   [1]Matt. 16:24

Always, and every hour; as well in small things as in great. I except nothing, but do desire that thou be found divested of all things.

Otherwise how canst thou be mine, and I thine, unless thou be stripped of all self-will, both within and without?

The sooner thou doest this, the better it will be with thee; and the more fully and sincerely thou doest it, so much the more shalt thou please Me, and so much the more shalt thou gain.

2. Some there are who resign themselves, but with certain exceptions: for they put not their whole trust in God, therefore, they study how to provide for themselves.

Some also at first offer all, but afterward being assailed with temptation, they return again to their own place, and therefore they make no progress in the path of virtue.

These shall not attain to the true liberty of a pure heart, nor to the grace of my sweetest familiarity, unless they first make an entire resignation and a daily sacrifice of themselves unto me. For without this, there neither is nor can be a fruitful union with Me.

3. I have very often said unto thee, and now again I say the same, Forsake thyself,[2] resign thyself, and thou shalt enjoy much inward peace.

---

[2]Matt. 16:24

Give all for all; seek nothing, require back nothing; abide purely and with a firm confidence in me, and thou shalt possess Me; thou shalt be free in heart, and darkness shalt not weigh thee down.

Let this be thy whole endeavor, let this be thy prayer, this thy desire; that being stripped of all selfishness, thou mayest with entire simplicity follow Jesus only, and dying to thyself mayest live eternally to Me.

Then shall all vain imaginations, evil disturbances, and superfluous cares fly away.

Then also immoderate fear shall forsake thee, and inordinate love shall die.

CHAPTER 38

Of Good Government in Things External, and of Having Recourse to God in Dangers

My son, thou oughtest with all diligence to endeavor that in every place and action, and in all external actions, thou be inwardly free, and thoroughly master of thyself; and that all things be under thee, and not thou under them.

Thou must be lord and master of thy own actions, not as a servant or a hireling.

Rather thou shouldest be as a freed man and a true Hebrew, passing into the lot and freedom of the sons of God.

For they standing upon the things that are present, contemplate the things which are eternal.

They look on transitory things with the left eye, and with the right do behold the things of heaven.

Temporal things can not draw them to adhere to them; rather they draw temporal things to serve them, and this in such way as they are ordained by God, and appointed by the Great Work-master, who hath left nothing in his creation without due order.

2. If too thou stand steadfast in all circumstances, and do not evaluate the things which thou seest and hearest by the outward appearance, nor with a carnal eye; but presently in every affair dost enter with Moses into the Tabernacle[1] to ask counsel of the Lord; thou shalt sometimes hear the Divine answer, and shalt return instructed concerning many things, both present and to come.

For Moses had always recourse to the Tabernacle for the deciding of doubts and questions, and fled to the help of prayer, for support under dangers and the iniquity of men.

So oughtest thou in like manner to fly to the closet of thine heart,[2] very earnestly imploring the Divine favor.

For we read, that for this cause Joshua, and the children of Israel were deceived by the

---

[1]Exodus 33:9   [2]Matt. 6:6

Gibeonites, because they asked not counsel from the Lord,[3] but giving too lightly credit to their fair words, were deluded by their counterfeit piety.

CHAPTER 39

That a Man Should Not Be Fretful in Matters of Business

My son, always commit thy cause to Me, I will dispose well of it in due time.

Wait for my appointment, and thou shalt find it will be for thy good.

O Lord, I do most cheerfully commit all things unto thee, for my effort can avail little.

Would that I might not be too much set upon future events, but give myself up unhesitatingly to thy good pleasure.

2. My son, oftentimes a man vehemently pursues something he desireth, and when he hath arrived at it, he beginneth to be of another mind; for man's affections do not long continue fixed on one object but rather do urge him from one thing to another.

It is therefore no small advantage for a man to forsake himself even in the smallest things.

3. The true progress of a man consisteth in

---

[3]John 9:14

the denying of himself; and he that is thus self-denied, liveth in great liberty and security.

But the old enemy,[1] who always sets himself against all who are good, ceaseth at no time from tempting, but day and night lieth grievously in wait, to cast the unwary, if he can, into the snare of deceit.

Therefore "Watch ye, and pray," saith our Lord, "that ye enter not into temptation."[2]

CHAPTER 40

That Man Hath No Good of Himself, Nor Anything In Which He Can Glory

"Lord, what is man, that thou art mindful of him, or the son of man, that thou visitest him?"[1]

What hath man deserved that thou shouldest grant him thy grace.

O Lord, what cause have I to complain, if thou forsake me? or if thou doest not that which I desire, what can I justly say against thy judgment?

Surely this I may truly think and say: Lord, I am nothing, I can do nothing, I have nothing that is good of myself, but in all things I am

---

[1] 1 Pet. 5:8   [2] Matt. 26:41   [1] Psalm 8:4

defective, and continually tend to achieve nothing.

And unless thou help me, and inwardly instruct me, I must become altogether lukewarm and ineffective.

2. But thou, O Lord, art always the same, and endurest for ever;[2] always Good, Just, and Holy, doing all things well, justly, and holily, and disposing all things with wisdom.

But I, who am more ready to go backward than forward, do not ever continue in one estate, for "seven different times are passed over me."[3]

Yet doth it soon become better, when it so pleaseth thee, and when thou dost agree to stretch forth thy helping hand; for thou canst help me alone without human aid, and so strengthen me, that my countenance shall be no more changed, but my heart shall be turned to thee alone, and be at rest.

3. Wherefore, if I could once perfectly cast off all human comfort, either for the attainment of devotion, or because of mine own necessities, which enforce me to seek after thee for no mortal man can comfort me, then might I well hope in thy grace, and rejoice for the gift of new consolation.

4. Thanks be unto thee, from whom all proceedeth, whensoever it goes well with me.

---

[2]Psalm 102:12   [3]Dan. 4:16, 23, 32

But I am in thy sight mere vanity and nothing, an inconstant and weak man.

Wherefore then can I glory? or for what do I desire to be respected? is it for being nothing? yet this is most vain.

Mere empty glory is in truth an evil plague, a very great vanity; because it draweth a man from true glory, and robbeth him of heavenly grace.

For whilst he pleaseth himself, he displeaseth thee; whilst he panteth after the praise of men, he is deprived of true virtues.

5. But the true glory and holy exultation is for a man to glory in thee,[4] and not in himself; to rejoice in thy name, not in his own virtue or strength, and not to find pleasure in any creature but for thy sake.

Praised be thy name, not mine; magnified be thy work, not mine. Let thy holy name be blessed, but to me let no part of men's praises be given.[5]

Thou art my glory, thou art the joy of my heart.

In thee will I glory and rejoice all the day, but as for myself, I will not glory, but in mine infirmities.

6. Let the Jews seek honor from one another,[6] I will seek that which cometh from God alone.

---

[4]Hab. 3:18   [5]Psalm 113:3; 115:1   [6]John 5:44

For all human glory, all temporal honor, all worldly elevation, compared to thy eternal glory, is vanity and folly.

O my God, my Truth, and my Mercy, O Blessed Trinity, to thee alone be praise, honor, power, and glory, for ever and ever.

CHAPTER 41

Of the Contempt of All Temporal Honor

My son make it no matter of thine, if thou see others honored and advanced, and thyself despised and debased.

Lift up thy heart into heaven to Me, and the contempt of men on earth will not grieve thee.

Lord, we are in blindness, and are quickly misled with vanity.

If I look well into myself, I can not say that any creature hath done me wrong; and therefore I can not justly complain against thee.

2. But because I have often and grievously sinned against thee, all creatures do justly take arms against me.

Unto me, therefore, shame and contempt is justly due, but unto thee praise, honor, and glory.

And unless I prepare myself with cheerful

willingness to be despised and forsaken of all creatures, and to be esteemed altogether nothing, I can not obtain inward peace and stability, nor be spiritually enlightened, nor be fully united unto thee.

CHAPTER 42

That Our Peace Is Not to Be Placed in Men

My son, if thou rest thy peace on any person because of the opinion which thou hast of him, or on account of thine intimate acquaintance with him, thou shalt ever be in an insecure and an entangled condition.

But if thou have recourse unto the ever-living and abiding Truth, the departure or death of a friend will not grieve thee.

The regard of thy friend ought to be grounded in Me; and for Me is he to be beloved, whoever he is whom thou thinkest well of, and who is very dear unto thee in this life.

Without Me no friendship can endure, or will continue; neither is that love true and pure, which is not bound together by Me.

Thou oughtest to be so dead to such affections of beloved friends, that, as much as concerns thee, thou shouldest wish to be without all company of men.

Man approacheth so much the nearer unto God, the further off he departeth from all earthly consolation.

In proportion, too, as he descendeth lower into himself, and is meaner in his own estimation, so much the higher he ascendeth unto God.

But he that attributeth any good unto himself, hindereth the coming of God's grace into him; for the grace of the Holy Spirit, ever seeketh an humble heart.[1]

If thou knowest perfectly how to annihilate thyself, and empty thyself of all created love, then should I flow into thee with great abundance of grace.

When thou lookest to the creatures, the sight of the Creator is withdrawn from thee.

Learn in all things to overcome thyself, for the love of thy Creator, and then shalt thou be able to attain to divine knowledge.

How small soever anything be, if it be inordinately loved and regarded, it keeps thee back from the chief good, and injures thy soul.

CHAPTER 43

Against Vain and Secular Knowledge

My son, let not the sayings of men move thee, however beautiful and subtle they may be. "For

---

[1] 1 Pet. 5:5

the kingdom of God consisteth not in word, but in power."[1]

Attend well to my words, for they inflame the heart, and enlighten the mind; they cause compunction, and they supply abundant variety of consolation.

Never read the Word in order to appear more learned or more wise.

Be studious for the mortification of thy sins; for this will profit thee more than the knowledge of many difficult questions.

2. When thou shalt have read and known many things, thou oughtest ever to return to one Beginning and Principle.

I am He that teacheth man knowledge; and I give unto little children a clearer understanding than can be taught by man.

He, therefore, to whom I speak, shall quickly be wise, and shall profit much in the spirit.

Woe to them that inquire many curious things of men, and little care about the way of serving Me!

The time will come, when the Master of masters shall appear, Christ the Lord of angels, to hear the lessons of all, that is, to examine the consciences of every one.

And then will he search Jerusalem with lamps, and the hidden things of darkness shall be brought to light,[2] and the arguings of men's tongues shall be silent.

---

[1] 1 Cor. 4:20   [2] Zeph. 1:12; 1 Cor. 4:5

3. I am He who in one instant do raise up the humble mind, to understand more of eternal truth, than if one had studied ten years in the schools.

I teach without noise of words, without confusion of opinions, without ambition of honor, without the scuffling of arguments.

I am He who instruct men to despise earthly things, to loathe things present, to seek things eternal, to relish things eternal; to flee honors, to suffer injuries, to place all hope in Me, to desire nothing from Me, and above all things ardently to love Me.

4. For a certain person, by loving Me fully, learned divine things, and spake that which was admirable.

He profited more by forsaking all things, than by studying subtilties.

But to some men I speak common things, to others things more particular; to some I appear sweetly by signs and figures, but to some I reveal mysteries with much light.

The voice of books is indeed one, but it instructs not all alike: for I am the teacher of the truth within, I am the searcher of the heart, the discerner of the thoughts, the mover of good actions, distributing to every man as I judge best.

CHAPTER 44

Of Not Fetching Trouble to Ourselves
From Outward Things

My son, in many things it is thy duty to be ignorant, and to esteem thyself as dead upon earth, and as one to whom the whole world is crucified.[1]

It is thy duty also to pass by many things with a deaf ear, and rather to think of those which belong unto thy peace.

It is more useful to turn away one's eyes from unpleasant things, and to leave every one to his own opinion, than to be a slave to contentious discourses.

If all things stand well between thee and God, and if thou hast his judgment in thy mind, thou shalt the more easily endure being overcome.

2. O Lord, to what a pass are we come! Behold, we bewail a temporal loss, for a small gain we toil and run; and the spiritual damage of our soul is forgotten, and hardly ever returns to the memory.

That which little or nothing profiteth, is minded, and that which is especially necessary, is slightly passed over; because the whole man doth sink into external things; and, unless he speedily repent, he settleth down in them, and that willingly.

---

[1]Gal. 6:14

CHAPTER 45

*That Credit Is Not to Be Given to All, and That
Man Is Prone to Offend in Words*

Grant me help, O Lord, in my tribulation, for
vain is the help of man![1]

How often have I been deceived, finding want
of faithfulness where I thought it sure!

And how often have I found it, where
beforehand I least expected it!

It is vain therefore to trust in men, but the
salvation of the righteous is in thee, O God!

Blessed be thou, O Lord, my God, in all
things that befall us.

We are weak and unsteadfast; we are quickly
deceived, and soon changed.

2. Who is he that is able in all things so
warily and circumspectly to keep himself, as
never to fall into any deceit or perplexity?

But he that trusteth in thee, O Lord, and
seeketh thee with a single heart, doth not so
easily fail.[2]

And if he fall into any tribulation, however
much he is entangled, yet he shall quickly either
through thee be delivered, or by thee be
comforted; for him that trusteth in thee, thou
wilt not forsake, even to the end.

A friend is rare to be found, that continueth
faithful in all his friend's distresses.

---

[1]Psalm 60:11   [2]Prov. 10:29

Thou, O Lord, even thou alone art most faithful at all times, and there is none like unto thee.

3. Oh, how wise was that holy soul that said, "My mind is firmly settled and grounded in Christ."

If it were so with me, then would not human fear easily vex me, nor the arrows of human words move me.

Who can foresee all things? Who is able to prepare beforehand for future evils? If things even foreseen do oftentimes hurt us, how can things unlooked for do otherwise than wound us grievously?

But wretch as I am, why did I not provide better for myself? Why also have I so easily had confidence in others?

But we are men, nothing else but frail men, although by many we are esteemed and called angels.

To whom shall I give credit, Lord? to whom but to thee? Thou art the truth, which neither doth deceive, nor can be deceived.

And on the other side, "every man is a liar,"[3] weak, inconstant, and subject to fall, especially in words; and therefore we must not easily give credit even to that which in outward show seemeth at the first to be right.

4. O with what wisdom hast thou warned us to beware of men; and because a man's foes are

------

[3]Rom. 3:4

they of his own household;[4] do not believe it, if one should say, "Behold here," or "Behold there."

Injury has been my instructor, and I wish it may make me more cautious and less simple.

"Be wary," saith one, "be wary, keep to thyself what I tell thee;" and while I hold my peace, and think it is secret, he can not himself keep that which he desired me to keep, but presently betrays both me and himself, and is gone.

From such tales and such indiscreet persons protect me, O Lord, that I neither fall into their hands, nor ever commit such things myself.

Grant me to observe truth and constancy in my words, and to remove far from me a crafty tongue.

What I am not willing to suffer in others, I ought by all means to avoid myself.

5. Oh how good is it and tending to peace, to be silent about other men, and not to believe promiscuously all that is said, nor easily to report what we have heard.[5]

Also it is good to lay one's self open to few, and always to be seeking after thee, who art the beholder of the heart.[6]

Nor should we be carried about with every wind of words, but desire that all things, both within and without, be accomplished according to the pleasure of thy will.

---

[4]Mic. 7:5   [5]Prov. 25:9   [6]Isaiah 26:3

How safe is it for the keeping of heavenly grace, to avoid appearances, and not to seek those things that seem to cause admiration abroad, but to pursue with all diligence the things which bring amendment of life and zeal of godliness.

6. To how many hath virtue known and over-hastily commended, been hurtful!

How profitable hath grace been when preserved in silence, in this frail life, which is said to be all temptation, and warfare!

CHAPTER 46

Of Putting Our Trust in God When Evil Words Arise

My son, stand steadily, and put thy trust in Me,[1] for what are words but words?

They fly through the air, but hurt not so much as a stone.

If thou art guilty, think that thou art most willing to amend thyself; if conscience reproach thee not, resolve to suffer this willingly for God's sake.

It is but a small matter to suffer sometimes a few words, if thou hast not yet the courage to endure hard blows.

---

[1]Psalm 37:3

And why do such small matters go to thy heart, but because thou art yet carnal, and regardest men more than thou oughtest?

For because thou art afraid to be despised, therefore thou wilt not be reproved for thy faults, and seekest the shelter of excuses.

2. But look better into thyself, and thou shalt see that the world is yet alive in thee, and a vain desire to please men.

For when thou shunnest the being humbled and reproved for thy faults, it is evident thou art neither truly humble, nor truly dead to the world, nor the world crucified to thee.

But give diligent ear to my words, and thou shalt not regard ten thousand words spoken by men.

Behold, if all should be spoken against thee that could be most maliciously invented, what would it hurt thee, if thou sufferedst it to pass and madest no more reckoning of it than of a straw? Could all those words pluck as much as one hair from thy head?[2]

3. But he that hath no heart in him, nor hath God before his eyes, is easily moved with a word of dispraise.

Whereas he that trusteth in Me, and affects not to confide in his own judgment, shall be free from the fear of men.

For I am the Judge[3] and the discerner of all secrets: I know how the matter passed; I know

---

[2]Matt. 10:30; Luke 12:7   [3]Psalm 7:8

him that offereth the injury, and him that suffereth it.

From me hath this proceeded; this hath happened by my permission, that the thoughts of many hearts may be revealed.[4]

I shall judge the guilty, and the innocent; but by a secret judgment I would beforehand try them both.

4. The testimony of men oftentimes deceiveth; but my judgment is true, it shall stand and not be overthrown.

It is commonly hidden, and not known in everything, but to few; notwithstanding it never erreth, neither can it err, although to the eyes of the foolish it seems not right.

Men ought therefore to have recourse to me in every judgment, and not to lean to their own judgment.

For the just man will not be troubled[5] whatsoever befalleth him from God; and if anything be wrongfully brought forth against him, he will not much care.

Neither will he vainly be glad, if by others he be with reason excused.

For he considereth that I am he that searcheth the heart and reins,[6] and do judge not according to the outward face, nor human appearance.

For that is oftentimes found blameworthy in my sight, which in the judgment of men is thought to be commendable.

---

[4]Luke 2:35　　[5]Prov. 12:13　　[6]Psalm 7:9; Rev. 2:23

O Lord God, the just Judge, strong and patient, thou who knowest the frailty and wickedness of men, be thou my strength, and all my trust, for mine own conscience sufficeth me not.

Although I know nothing by myself,[7] yet I can not hereby justify myself; for without thy mercy, in thy sight shall no man living be justified.[8]

CHAPTER 47

That All Grievous Things Are to Be Endured For the Sake of Eternal Life

My son, be not dismayed with the painful labors which thou hast undertaken for Me, neither be thou utterly cast down because of any tribulations which befall thee; but let my promise strengthen and comfort thee under every circumstance.

I am well able to reward thee, above all measure and degree.

Thou shalt not long toil here, nor always be pressed with griefs.

Wait a little while, and thou shalt see a speedy end of thine evils.

There will come an hour when all labor and trouble shall cease.

---

[7]1 Cor 4:4   [8]Psalm 143:2

Poor and brief is all that which passeth away with time.

2. Do in earnest what thou doest; labor faithfully in my vineyard;[1] I will be thy reward.

Write, read, chant, mourn, keep silence, pray, suffer crosses manfully; life everlasting is worthy of all these, yea, and greater combats.

Peace shall come in one day which is known unto the Lord, and it shall be not day nor night,[2] that is, of this present time, but everlasting light, infinite brightness, steadfast peace, and secure rest.

Then thou shalt not say, "Who shall deliver me from the body of this death?"[3] nor cry, "Woe is me, that my sojourning is prolonged!"[4] for death shall be cast down headlong, and there shall be salvation which can not fail, no more anxiety, but blessed joy, sweet and glorious society.

3. Oh! if thou hadst seen the everlasting crowns of the saints in heaven,[5] and with how great glory they now rejoice, who in times past appeared contemptible to this world, and esteemed unworthy of life itself; truly thou wouldest presently humble thyself even unto the earth, and wouldest rather seek to be in subjection to all, than to have command so much as over one.

Neither wouldest thou desire the pleasant

---

[1]Matt. 20:7   [2]Zech. 14:7   [3]Rom. 7:24
[4]Psalm 120:5   [5]Wisd. 3:1-9; 5:16

days of this life, but rather rejoice to suffer affliction for God's sake and esteem it thy greatest gain to be reputed as nothing amongst men.

4. Oh, if thou hadst a relishing of these things, and didst allow them to sink into the bottom of thy heart, how wouldst thou so much as once to complain?

Are not all painful labors to be endured for the sake of life eternal?

It is no small matter to lose or to gain the kingdom of God.

Lift up thy face therefore unto heaven; behold I and all my saints with Me, who in this world had great conflicts, do now rejoice, are now comforted, now secure, now at rest, and shall remain with Me everlastingly in the kingdom of my Father.

CHAPTER 48

Of the Day of Eternity and This Life's Straitnesses

O, most blessed mansion of the city which is above;[1] O, most clear day of eternity, which no night obscureth, but the highest Truth ever enlighteneth; O, day ever joyful, ever secure, and never changing into a contrary state!

---

[1]Rev. 21:2

Oh, that that day might once appear, and that all these temporal things were at an end!

To the saints it shineth glowing with everlasting brightness, but to those that are pilgrims on the earth, it appeareth only afar off, and as it were through a glass.

2. The citizens of heaven do know how joyful that day is, but the exiled children of Eve bewail the bitterness and tediousness of this.

The days of this life are short and evil,[2] full of sorrow, and distresses.

Here a man is defiled with many sins, insnared with many passions, held fast by many fears, harassed with many cares, distracted with many curiosities, entangled with many vanities, compassed about with many errors, worn away with many labors, burdened with temptations, enervated by pleasures, tormented with want.

3. Oh, when shall these evils be at an end? when shall I be delivered from the miserable bondage of my sins?[3] when shall I think, O Lord, of thee alone?[4] when shall I fully rejoice in thee?

When shall I enjoy true liberty without any impediments whatsoever, without any trouble of mind and body?

When shall I have solid peace, peace secure and undisturbed, peace within and peace without, peace every way assured?

O merciful Jesu, when shall I stand to behold

---

[2]Job 7   [3]Rom. 7:24   [4]Psalm 71:16

thee? when shall I contemplate the glory of thy kingdom? when wilt thou be unto me all in all?

Oh, when shall I be with thee in thy kingdom, which thou hast prepared for thy beloved from all eternity?

I am left, a poor and banished man, in the land of mine enemies, where there are daily wars and great misfortunes.

4. Comfort my banishment, assuage my sorrow; for my whole desire sigheth after thee.

For all is burdensome to me whatsoever this world offereth for my consolation.

I long to enjoy thee most inwardly, but I can not attain unto it.

My desire is, that I may be wholly given up to things heavenly, but temporal things and unmortified passions weigh me down.

With the mind I wish to be above all things, but with the flesh I am enforced against my will to be subject to them.

Thus, unhappy man that I am,[5] I fight with myself, and am become burdensome to myself, while my spirit seeketh to be above, and my flesh to be below.

5. Oh, what do I inwardly suffer, when in my mind I dwell on things heavenly, and presently, while I pray, a multitude of carnal fancies occur to me! O my God! be not thou far from me, nor turn away in wrath from thy servant.[6]

---

[5]Rom. 7:24; 8:23   [6]Psalm 72:12

Cast forth thy lightning, and disperse them: shoot out thine arrows, and let all the imaginations of the enemy be put to flight.

Gather in, and call home my senses unto thee; make me to forget all worldly things; enable me to cast away speedily, and with scorn, all vicious imaginations.

Succor me, O thou the everlasting Truth, that no vanity may move me.

Come to me, thou heavenly sweetness, and let all impurity flee from before thy face.

Pardon me also, and in mercy deal gently with me, as often as in prayer I think on nothing beside thee.

I must truly confess that I am wont to be subject to many distractions.

For many, many times I am not there, where I am bodily standing, or sitting, but rather I am there, whither my thoughts do carry me.

Where my thoughts are, there am I; and commonly there are my thoughts, where my affection is.

That too readily occurs to me, which is naturally delightsome, or by custom is pleasing.

6. And for this cause thou that art truth itself hast plainly said, "Where thy treasure is, there is also thy heart."[7]

If I love heaven, I willingly think on heavenly things.

If I love the world, I rejoice at the prosperity

---

[7]Matt. 6:31

of the world, and grieve for the adversity thereof.

If I love the flesh, I shall fancy oftentimes those things that are pleasing to the flesh.

If I love the spirit, I shall delight to think on things spiritual.

For whatsoever I love, thereof do I willingly speak and hear, and carry home with me the forms thereof.

But blessed is the man,[8] who, for thy sake, O Lord, is willing to abandon all creatures, who does violence to his nature, and through fervor of spirit crucifieth the lusts of the flesh; that so with a serene conscience he may offer pure prayers unto thee, and all earthly things, both outwardly and inwardly, being excluded, he may be fit to be admitted into the angelical choirs.

CHAPTER 49

Of the Desire of Everlasting Life, and How Great Rewards Are Promised to Those That Strive Resolutely

My son when thou perceivest the desire of everlasting bliss to be given thee from above, and desirest to depart out of the tabernacle of this body, that thou mayest contemplate my brightness without shadow of turning; open thy

---

[8] Matt. 19

heart wide, and receive this holy inspiration with thy whole desire.

Give greatest thanks to the heavenly goodness, which dealeth with thee so favorably, visiting thee mercifully, stirring thee up fervently, powerfully holding thee up, lest through thine own weight thou fall down to the things of earth.

Neither dost thou obtain this by thine own thought or endeavor, but by the mere condescension of heavenly grace and divine favor; to the end that thou mayest make further progress in all virtue, and obtain greater humility, and prepare thyself for future conflicts, and endeavor to cleave unto Me with the whole affection of thy heart, and to serve Me with fervent desire.

2. My son, oftentimes the fire burneth, but the flame ascendeth not up without smoke.

So likewise the desires of some men burn toward heavenly things, and yet they are not free from temptation of carnal affection.

And therefore it is not altogether purely for the honor of God, that they make such earnest requests to him.

Such also oftentimes are thy desires, which thou hast pretended to be so serious and earnest.

For those are not pure and perfect desires, which are alloyed with thine own special interest and advantage.

3. Ask not that which is delightful and profitable to thee, but that which is acceptable to Me, and tends to promote my honor; for if

thou judgest rightly, thou oughtest to prefer and follow my appointment, rather than thine own desire, or any desired thing whatever.

I know thy desire, and have heard thy frequent groanings.

Now thou longest to enjoy the glorious liberty of the sons of God; now doth the everlasting dwelling, and the heavenly country replenished with all joy, delight thee; but that hour is not yet come; as yet there is another time, and that a time of war,[1] a time of labor and of probation.

Thou desirest to be filled with the sovereign Good, but thou canst not attain it for the present.

I am he; wait thou for me, saith the Lord, until the kingdom of God doth come.

4. Thou art yet to be tried upon earth, and to be exercised in many things.

Consolation shall be sometimes given thee, but the abundant fulness thereof shall not be granted.

Take courage, therefore, and be valiant[2] as well in doing as in suffering things contrary to nature.

Thou oughtest to put on the new man,[3] and to be changed into another person.

It is often thy duty to do that which thou wouldest not, and to leave undone what thou wouldest do.

---

[1]Job 7:1   [2]Joshua 1:7   [3]Eph. 4:24

That which is pleasing to others, shall prosper; that which thou wishest, shall not speed.

That which others say, shall be heard; what thou sayest, shall be accounted nothing; others shall ask and shall receive; thou shalt ask but shalt not obtain.

5. Others shall be great in the praise of men, but about thee there shall be nothing said.

To others this or that shall be committed, but thou shalt be accounted a thing of no use.

At this nature will sometimes be troubled, and it is much if thou bearest it with silence.

In these and many such-like instances, the faithful servant of the Lord is wont to be tried, how he can deny and break himself in all things.

There is scarcely anything wherein thou hast such need to die to thyself, as in seeing and suffering those things that are contrary to thy will; especially when that is commanded which seemeth unto thee inconvenient, or less profitable.

And because thou, being under authority darest not resist the higher power, therefore it seems hard to thee to walk at the command of another, and to let go all thine own opinion.

6. But consider, my son, the fruit of these labors, the end near at hand, and the reward exceeding great; and thou wilt not be reluctant to bear them, rather thou wilt take great comfort of thy patience.

For even instead of that little of thy will,

which now thou readily forsakest, thou shalt always have thy will in heaven.

Yea, there thou shalt find all that thou mayest wish, all that thou shalt be able to desire.

There thou shalt have within thy reach all good, without fear of losing it.

There shall thy will be ever one with Me; it shall not covet any outward or private thing.

There none shall withstand thee, no man shall complain of thee, no man hinder thee, nothing come in thy way; but all things desired shall be there together present, and refresh thy whole affection, and fill it up to the brim.

There I will give thee glory for the reproach which here thou sufferedst, the garment of praise for heaviness, for the lowest place a kingly throne for ever.

There shall the fruit of obedience appear, the labor of repentance rejoice, and humble subjection shall be gloriously crowned.

7. At present then bend thyself humbly under all, and care not who said or commanded this.

But take great care, that whether thy superior, or thy inferior, or thine equal, require anything of thee, or even insinuate their desire, thou take it all in good part, and with a sincere will endeavor to fulfil it.

Let one seek this, another that; let this man glory in this thing, the other in that, and be praised a thousand thousand times; but do thou rejoice neither in this, nor in that, but in the contempt of thyself, and in the good pleasure and honor of Me alone.

This is what thou art to wish, that God may be always glorified in thee, whether it be by life or in death.

CHAPTER 50

How a Desolate Person Ought to Offer Himself Into the Hands of God

O Lord God, Holy Father, be thou blessed both now and for evermore, because as thou wilt, so is it done, and what thou doest is always good.

Let thy servant rejoice in thee, not in himself nor in anything else; for thou alone art the true gladness, thou art my hope and my crown, thou art my joy and my honor, O Lord.

What hath thy servant, but what he hath received from thee,[1] even without any merit of his own?

Thine are all things, both what thou hast given, and what thou hast made.

I am poor, and in labors, from my youth;[2] and sometimes my soul is sorrowful even unto tears; sometimes also it is disturbed within itself by reason of impending sufferings.

2. I long after the joy of peace, I earnestly crave the peace of thy children who are fed by thee in the light of thy consolation.

---

[1] 1 Cor. 4:7   [2] Psalm 88:15

If thou give peace, if thou pour into my heart holy joy, the soul of thy servant shall be full of melody, and shall become devout in thy praise.

But if thou withdraw thyself, as too many times thou doest, he will not be able to run in the way of thy commandments; but rather he will bow his knees, and smite his breast, because it is not now with him as it was in times past, when thy lamp shone upon his head, and under the shadow of thy wings he was protected from the temptations which assaulted him.

3. O righteous Father, and ever to be praised, the hour is come that thy servant is to be proved.

O beloved Father, just and right it is that in this hour thy servant should suffer something for thy sake.

O Father, evermore to be honored, the hour is come, which from all eternity thou didst foreknow should come; that for a short time thy servant should outwardly be oppressed, but inwardly should ever live with thee.

It is well that he should be for a little while held cheap and humbled, and in the sight of men should fail, and be wasted with sufferings and weakness, that he may rise again with thee in the morning dawn of the light, and be glorified in heaven.

Holy Father, thou hast so appointed it and so wilt have it; and that is fulfilled which thyself hast commanded.

4. For this is a favor to thy friend, that he

may suffer and be afflicted in the world for love of thee, however often by and whoever thou permittest it to fall upon him.

Without thy counsel and providence, and without cause, nothing cometh to pass in the earth.

It is good for me, Lord, that thou hast humbled me,[3] that I may learn thy righteous judgments, and may cast away all pride of heart, and all presumptuousness.

It is profitable for me, that shame hath covered my face, that I may seek from thee my consolation rather than from men.

I have learned also hereby to fear thy unsearchable judgments, who afflictest the just with the wicked, though not without equity and justice.

5. I give thee thanks, that thou hast not spared my sins, but hast bruised me with bitter stripes, inflicting sorrows, and sending anxieties upon me within and without.

There is none else under heaven who can comfort me, but thou only, O Lord my God, the Heavenly Physician of souls, who woundest and healest, who bringest down to hell and bringest back again.[4]

Thy discipline shall be over me, and thy rod itself shall instruct me.

6. Behold, O beloved Father, I am in thy

---

[3] Psalm 119:71   [4] Tob. 13:2; Psalm 18:16

hands, I bow myself under the rod of thy correction.

Strike my back and my neck too, that my perversity may be conformed to thy will.

Make me a dutiful and humble disciple of thine as thou art well wont to do; that I may be ready at every demand of thy divine pleasure.

Unto thee I commend myself and all mine to be corrected; it is better to be punished here, than hereafter.

Thou knowest all things generally, and also each separately, and there is nothing in man's conscience which can be hidden from thee.

Before things are done, thou knowest that they will come to pass, and hast no need that any should teach thee, or admonish thee of those things which are being done on the earth.

Thou knowest what is expedient for my spiritual progress, and how greatly tribulation serves to scour off the rust of my sins.

Do with me according to thy desired good pleasure, and disdain me not for my sinful life, known to none so thoroughly and clearly as to thee alone.

7. Grant me, O Lord, to know that which is worth knowing, to love that which is worth loving, to praise that which pleaseth thee most, to esteem that which is precious unto thee, to despise that which in thy sight is contemptible.

Suffer me not to judge according to the sight of the outward eyes, nor to give sentence according to the hearing of the ears of ignorant men; but with a true judgment to discern between things visible and spiritual, and above all to be ever searching after the good pleasure of thy will.

8. The minds of men are often deceived in their judgments; the lovers of the world too are deceived in loving only things visible.

How is a man ever better, for being esteemed great by man?

The deceitful in flattering the deceitful, the vain man in extolling the vain, the blind in commending the blind, the weak in magnifying the weak, deceiveth him; and verily doth more shame him, while he doth vainly praise him.

"For what every one is in thy sight, that is he, and no more," saith humble St. Francis.

CHAPTER 51

That a Man Ought to Employ Himself in Works of Humility, When Strength Is Wanting for Higher Employments

My son, thou art not able always to continue in the more fervent desire of virtue, nor to persist in the higher degree of contemplation; but thou must sometimes of necessity by reason of original corruption descend to inferior things, and bear the burden of this corruptible life, though against thy will, and with wearisomeness.

As long as thou carriest a mortal body, thou shalt feel weariness and heaviness of heart.

Thou oughtest therefore while in the flesh oftentimes to bewail the burden of the flesh; for that thou canst not always continue in spiritual exercises and divine contemplations.

2. It is then expedient for thee to flee to humble and exterior works, and to refresh thyself with good actions, to expect with a firm confidence my coming and heavenly visitation, to bear patiently thy banishment and the dryness of thy mind, till I shall again visit thee and set thee free from all anxieties.

For I will cause thee to forget thy former pains, and to enjoy thorough inward quietness.

I will lay open before thee the pleasant fields of Holy Scripture that with an enlarged heart thou mayest begin to run the way of my commandments.

And thou shalt say, "The sufferings of this present time are not worthy to be compared with the future glory that shall be revealed in us."[1]

CHAPTER 52

That a Man Ought Not to Account Himself as Worthy of Comfort, But Rather as Deserving of Chastisement

O Lord, I am not worthy of thy consolation, nor of any spiritual visitation; and therefore thou

---

[1]Romans 8:18

dealest justly with me, when thou leavest me poor and desolate.

For though I could shed a sea of tears, yet should I not be worthy of thy consolation.

Wherefore I deserve nothing but to be scourged and punished, in that I have grievously and often offended thee, and in many things have sinned greatly.

All things therefore duly considered, I am not worthy even of the least consolation.

But thou, O gracious and merciful God, who wilt not that thy works should perish, to show the riches of thy goodness upon the vessels of mercy, grantest even beyond all his deserving to comfort thy servant above the manner of men.

For thy consolations are not like to the discourses of men.

2. What have I done, O Lord, that thou shouldest bestow any heavenly comfort upon me?

I remember not that I have done any good, but have been always prone to sin, and slow to amendment.

This is true, and I can not deny it: if I should say otherwise thou wouldest stand against me,[1] and there would be none to defend me.

What have I deserved for my sins, but hell and everlasting fire?

I confess in very truth that I am worthy of all scorn and contempt, nor is it fit that I should be remembered among thy devout servants.

---

[1] Job 9:2-3

And although I be unwilling to hear this, yet notwithstanding, for the truth's sake, I will lay open my sins against myself, that so the more speedily I may obtain mercy at thy hand.

3. What shall I say, in that I am guilty, and full of all confusion?

My mouth can utter nothing but this word only, "I have sinned, O Lord! I have sinned;[2] have mercy on me, pardon me."

Suffer me a little, that I may mourn my griefs, before I go into the land of darkness, a land covered with the shadow of death.[3]

What dost thou so much require of a guilty and miserable sinner, as that he be contrite, and that he humble himself for his sins?

Of true contrition and humbling of the heart, ariseth hope of forgiveness; the troubled conscience is reconciled to God; the favor of God, which was lost, is recovered; man is preserved from the wrath to come; and God and the penitent soul meet together with a holy kiss.

4. Humble contrition for sins is an acceptable sacrifice unto thee, O Lord,[4] savoring much sweeter in thy presence than the perfume of frankincense.

This is also the pleasant ointment,[5] which thou desirest should be poured upon thy sacred feet, for a contrite and humble heart thou never hast despised.[6]

Here is the place of refuge from the angry face

---

[2] Psalm 51   [3] Job 10:21   [4] Psalm 51:17
[5] Luke 7:38   [6] Psalm 51:17

of the enemy; here is amended and washed away, whatever defilement and pollution hath been elsewhere contracted.

CHAPTER 53

That the Grace of God Doth Not Join Itself With Those Who Cherish Earthly Things

My son, my grace is precious, it suffereth not itself to be mingled with external things, nor with earthly consolations.

Thou oughtest therefore to cast away all obstacles to grace, if thou desire to receive the infusion thereof.

Choose therefore a secret place to thyself, love to dwell alone with thyself, desire the conversation of none, but rather pour out devout prayer unto God, that thou mayest keep thy mind in compunction, and thy conscience pure.

Esteem thou the whole world as nothing; prefer attendance upon God before all outward things.

For thou wilt not be able to attend upon Me, and at the same time to take delight in things transitory.

Thou oughtest to remove thyself from thy acquaintance and friends,[1] and to keep thy mind void of all temporal comfort.

---

[1] Matt. 19:29

So the blessed apostle Peter beseecheth, that the faithful of Christ would keep themselves in the world as strangers and pilgrims.[2]

2. Oh, how great a confidence shall he have at the hour of death, whom no affection to any earthly thing detaineth in the world.

But the having a heart so retired from all, the sickly mind doth not as yet comprehend; nor doth the carnal man know the liberty of the spiritual man.

Notwithstanding, if he will be truly spiritual, he ought to renounce as well those who are far off, as those who are near unto him, and to beware of no man more than of himself.

If thou perfectly overcome thyself, thou shalt very easily bring all else under the yoke.

The perfect victory is to triumph over ourselves.

For he that keepeth himself subject in such sort that his sensual affections be obedient to reason, and his reason in all things obedient to Me; that person is truly conqueror of himself, and lord of the world.

3. If thou desire to mount unto this height, thou must set out courageously, and lay the axe to the root, that thou mayest pluck up and destroy both that hidden inordinate inclination to self, and all {love of} private and earthly good.

On this sin that man too inordinately loveth himself almost all dependeth, whatsoever is

---

[2] 1 Pet. 2:11

thoroughly to be overcome; which evil being once vanquished and subdued, there will presently ensue great peace and tranquillity.

But because few endeavor perfectly to die unto themselves, and altogether to go out of themselves, therefore they remain entangled in themselves, and can not be elevated in spirit above themselves.

But he that desireth to walk freely with Me, it is necessary that he mortify all perverse and inordinate affections, and that he should not earnestly adhere unto any creature with particular love.

CHAPTER 54

Of the Different Motions of Nature and Grace

My son, mark diligently the motions of nature and grace; for in a very contrary and subtile manner these are moved, and can hardly be discerned but by him that is spiritually and inwardly enlightened.

All men indeed desire that which is good, and pretend some good in their words and deeds; and therefore under the appearance of good, many are deceived.

Nature is crafty, and seduceth many, entangleth and deceiveth them, and always proposeth herself for her end and object.

But grace walketh in simplicity, abstaineth

from all appearance of evil, pretendeth not deceits, and doeth all things purely for God's sake, in whom also she finally resteth.

2. Nature will not willingly die, nor be kept down, nor be overcome, nor be subject to any, nor be subdued without reluctance:

But grace studieth self-mortification, resisteth sensuality, seeketh to be subject, is willing to be kept under, nor wishes to use her own liberty; she loves to be kept under discipline, and desires not to rule over any, but always to live and remain and be under God, and for God's sake is ready humbly to bow down unto all mankind.

Nature striveth for her own advantage, and considereth what profit she may reap by another:

Grace considereth not what is profitable and commodious unto herself, but rather what may be for the good of many.

Nature willingly receiveth honor and respect:

But grace faithfully attributeth all honor and glory unto God.

3. Nature is afraid of shame and contempt:

But grace rejoiceth to suffer reproach for the name of Jesus.

Nature loveth leisure and bodily rest:

But grace can not be idle, but cheerfully embraceth labor.

Nature seeketh to have those things that be curious and beautiful, and abhorreth that which is cheap and coarse:

But grace delighteth in what is plain and

humble, despiseth not rough things, nor refuseth to wear that which is old and patched.

Nature hath regard to temporal things, rejoiceth at earthly gain, sorroweth for loss, is irritated by every little injurious word:

But grace attends to things eternal, cleaves not to things temporal, is not troubled with losses, nor disturbed with hard words; because she hath placed her treasure and joy in heaven, where nothing perisheth.

4. Nature is covetous, doth more willingly receive than give, and loveth to have things private and what she can call her own.

But grace is kind-hearted and communicative, shunneth private interest, is content with a little, judgeth that it is more blessed to give than to receive.

Nature inclines a man to the creatures, to his own body, to vanities, and to running to and fro:

But grace draweth unto God and to every virtue, renounceth creatures, avoideth the word, hateth the desires of the flesh, restraineth wanderings abroad, blusheth to be seen in public.

Nature is willing to have some outward comfort, wherein she may be sensibly delighted:

But grace seeketh consolation in God alone, and to have delight in the highest good above all visible things.

5. Nature manages everything for her own gain and profit, she can not bear to do anything

gratis, but for every kindness she hopes to obtain either what is equal, or what is better, or at least praise or favor; and is very earnest to have her works and gifts much valued:

But grace seeketh no temporal thing, nor desireth any other reward than God alone, nor asketh more of temporal necessaries, than what may serve her for the obtaining of things eternal.

6. Nature rejoiceth to have many friends and kinsfolk, she glorieth in her noble place and noble birth, smiles on the powerful, fawns upon the rich, applauds those who are like herself:

But grace loves even her enemies, and is not puffed up with a multitude of friends; nor thinks much of high birth, unless it be joined with more exalted virtue.

Grace favoreth the poor rather than the rich, hath more compassion for the innocent than for the powerful, rejoiceth with the true man, not with the deceitful.

She is ever exhorting good men to labor for the best gifts; and by all virtue to become like to the Son of God.

Nature quickly complaineth of want and trouble:

Grace endureth need with firmness and constancy.

7. Nature referreth all things to herself, striveth and contendeth for herself:

But grace bringeth back all to God, whence originally they proceed; she ascribeth no good to herself, nor doth she arrogantly presume, she contendeth not, nor preferreth her own opinion before others; but in every matter of sense and understanding submitteth herself unto the eternal wisdom and to the divine judgment.

Nature is eager to know secrets and to hear news; she likes to appear abroad, and to make proof of many things by her own senses; she desires to be noticed, and to do things for which she may be praised and admired:

But grace cares not to hear news, nor to understand curious matters; because all this takes its rise from the old corruption of man, since upon earth there is nothing new, nothing durable.

Grace teacheth therefore to restrain the senses, to shun vain complacency and ostentation, humbly to hide those things that are worthy of admiration and praise, and of everything, and in every knowledge, to seek profitable fruit, and the praise and honor of God.

She will not have herself nor what belongs to her praised, but desireth that God should be blessed in his gifts, who through mere love, bestoweth all things.

8. This grace is a supernatural light, and a certain special gift of God, and the proper mark of the elect, and pledge of everlasting salvation; it raiseth up a man from earthly things to love the things of heaven, and of a carnal maketh him a spiritual man.

The more therefore nature is kept down and

subdued, so much the greater grace is infused, and daily by new visitations the inward man becomes more reformed according to the image of God.

CHAPTER 55

Of the Corruption of Nature, and of the Efficacy of Divine Grace

O Lord, my God, who hast created me after thine own image and likeness,[1] grant me this grace, which thou hast showed to be so great and so necessary to salvation; that I may overcome my most evil nature, which draweth me to sin and to perdition.

For I feel in my flesh the law of sin contradicting the law of my mind[2] and leading me captive to the obeying of sensuality in many things; neither can I resist the passions thereof, unless thy most holy grace, fervently infused into my heart do assist me.

2. There is need of thy grace, O Lord, and of great degrees thereof, that nature may be overcome, which is ever prone to evil from her youth.[3]

For through Adam, the first man, nature being fallen and corrupted by sin the penalty of this stain hath descended upon all mankind, so that "nature" itself, which by thee was created good and upright, is now taken for the sin and

---

[1] Gen. 1:26   [2] Rom. 7:23   [3] Gen. 8:21

infirmity of corrupted nature; because the inclination thereof left unto itself draweth to evil and to inferior things.

For the small power which remaineth is as a spark lying hid in the ashes.

This is natural reason itself, encompassed about with great darkness, yet still retaining power to discern the difference between true and false, good and evil, although it be unable to fulfil all that it approveth, and enjoyeth no longer the full light of the truth, nor soundness of the affections.

3. Hence it is, O my God, that I delight in thy law after the inward man,[4] knowing thy commandment to be good, just and holy, reproving also all evil and sin, teaching that it is to be avoided.

But with the flesh I serve the law of sin, while I obey sensuality rather than reason.

Hence it is, that to will what is good is present with me, but how to accomplish it I find not.

Hence it is that I often purpose many good things, but because grace is wanting to help my weakness, upon a light resistance I start back and faint.

Hence it comes to pass that I know the way of perfection, and see clearly enough how I ought to act; but being pressed down with the weight of mine own corruption, I rise not to what is very perfect.

---

[4]Rom. 7:22

4. O Lord, how entirely needful is thy grace for me, to begin anything good, to proceed with it, and to accomplish it.

For without it I can do nothing,[5] but in thee I can do all things, when thy grace doth strengthen me.

Oh, grace truly celestial! without which our most worthy actions are nothing, nor are any gifts of nature to be esteemed.

Neither arts or riches, beauty or strength, genius or eloquence, are of any value before thee, without thy grace, O Lord.

For gifts of nature are common to good and bad, but the peculiar gift of the elect is grace and love; and they that bear this honorable mark, are accounted worthy of everlasting life.

So esteemed is this grace, that neither the gift of prophecy, nor the working of miracles, nor any speculation (however high) is of any esteem without it.

No, not even faith or hope, or any other virtues are unto thee acceptable without charity and grace.[6]

5. Oh, most blessed grace, that makest the poor in spirit rich in virtues, and renderest him who is rich in many goods humble in heart!

Come thou down unto me, come and replenish me early with thy comfort, lest my soul faint for weariness and dryness of mind.

I beseech thee, O Lord, that I may find grace in thy sight; for thy grace is sufficient for me,

---

[5]John 15:5   [6]1 Cor. 13:13

though other things that nature longeth for I obtain not.

Although I be tempted and vexed with many tribulations, yet I will fear no evils,[7] so long as thy grace is with me.

This alone is my strength; this alone giveth counsel and help.

This is stronger than all enemies, and wiser than all the wise.

6. The grace is the mistress of truth, the teacher of discipline, the light of the heart, the solace in affliction, the banisher of sorrow, the expeller of fear, the nurse of devotion, the mother of tears.

Without this, what am I but a withered branch, and an unprofitable trunk appropriate only to be cast away!

Let thy grace therefore, O Lord, always prevent and follow me, and make me to be continually given to good works, through thy Son Jesus Christ. Amen.

CHAPTER 56

That We Ought to Deny Ourselves and Imitate Christ By the Cross

My son, the more thou canst go out of thyself, so much the more wilt thou be able to enter into Me.

---

[7]Psalm 23:4

As to be void of all desire of external things, produceth inward peace, so the forsaking of ourselves inwardly, joineth us unto God.

I will have thee learn the perfect renunciation of thyself to my will, without contradiction or complaint.

Follow thou Me: "I am the Way, the Truth, and the Life."[1] Without the Way, there is no going; without the Truth there is no knowing; without the Life, there is no living. I am the Way, which thou oughtest to follow; the Truth, which thou oughtest to trust; the Life, which thou oughtest to hope for.

I am the inviolable Way, the infallible Truth, the endless Life.

I am the straightest Way, the sovereign Truth, the true, the blessed, the uncreated Life.

If thou abide in my way, thou shalt know the Truth, and the Truth shall make thee free, and thou shalt attain eternal life.

2. If thou wilt enter into life, keep the commandments.[2]

If thou wilt know the truth, believe Me.

If thou wilt be perfect, sell all.[3]

If thou wilt be my disciple, deny thyself.[4]

If thou wilt possess a blessed life, despise this present life.

If thou wilt be exalted in heaven, humble thyself in this world.[5]

---

[1]John 14:6   [2]Matt. 19:17   [3]Matt. 19:21
[4]Luke 9:23   [5]John 12:25

If thou wilt reign with Me, bear the cross with Me.[6]

For only the servants of the cross can find the way of blessedness and of true light.

3. O Lord Jesus, forasmuch as thy life is strict and despised by the world, grant me grace to imitate thee, though with the world's contempt.

For the servant is not greater than his lord,[7] nor the disciple above his master.

Let thy servant be exercised in thy life and conversation for therein my salvation and true holiness doth consist.

Whatsoever I read or hear besides it, doth not recreate nor give me full delight.

4. My son, now that thou knowest and hast read all these things, happy shalt thou be, if thou do them.

"He that hath my commandments and keepeth them, he it is that loveth Me; and I will love him, and will manifest myself unto him,"[8] and will make him sit together with Me in my Father's kingdom.

O Lord Jesu, as thou hast said and promised, so let it come to pass, and grant that I may not wholly undeserve this favor.

I have received the cross, I have received it from thy hand; I will bear it, and bear it even unto death, as thou hast laid it upon me.

---

[6]Luke 14:27   [7]Matt. 10:24; Luke 6:40   [8]John 14:21

Truly the life of a good religious person is a cross, yet is it also a guide to paradise.

It is now begun, it is not lawful to go back, neither is it fit to leave that which we have undertaken.

5. Let us then take courage, brethren, let us go forward together, Jesus will be with us.

For the sake of Jesus we have undertaken this cross, for the sake of Jesus let us persevere in the cross.

He will be our helper, who is also our guide and forerunner.

Behold, our king marcheth before us, and he will fight for us.

Let us follow manfully, let no man fear any terrors; let us be prepared to die valiantly in battle, nor bring such a disgrace on our glory as to flee from the cross.

CHAPTER 57

That a Man Should Not Be Too Much Dejected,
Even When He Falleth Into Some Defects

My son, patience and humility in adversities are more pleasing to Me, than much comfort and devotion in prosperities.

Why art thou so grieved for every little matter spoken against thee?

Although it had been much more, thou oughtest not to have been disturbed.

But now let it pass; it is not the first that hath

happened, nor is it anything new; neither shall it be the last, if thou live long.

Thou art courageous enough, so long as nothing adverse cometh thy way.

Thou canst give good counsel also, and canst encourage others with thy words; but when any tribulation suddenly comes to thy door, thou failest in counsel and in strength.

Observe then thy great frailty, of which thou too often hast experience in trifling occurrences.

It is notwithstanding intended for thy good, when these and such like things happen to thee.

2. Put it out of thy heart the best thou canst, and if it touch thee, yet let it not discourage thee, nor perplex thee long.

At least bear it patiently, if thou canst not joyfully.

Although thou be unwilling to hear it, and feelest indignation thereat, yet restrain thyself, and suffer no inordinate word to pass out of thy mouth, whereby Christ's little ones may be offended.

The storm which is now raised shall quickly be allayed, and inward grief shall be sweetened by returning grace.

I yet live, saith the Lord, and am ready to help thee,[1] and to give thee greater comfort than before, if thou put thy trust in me, and callest devoutly upon me.

3. Be more patient of soul, and gird thyself to greater endurance.

---

[1] Isaiah 69:18

All is not lost, although thou do feel thyself very often afflicted or grievously tempted.

Thou art a man, and not God; thou art flesh not an angel.

How canst thou continue always in the same state of virtue, when an angel in heaven hath fallen, as also the first man in paradise?[2]

I am He who will strengthen with health them that mourn, and do raise up unto divine glory those that know their own infirmity.

4. O Lord, blessed be thy word, more sweet unto my mouth than honey and the honey-comb.[3]

What should I do in these so great tribulations and necessities, unless thou didst comfort me with thy holy words?

What matter is it, how much or what I suffer, so as I may at length attain to the port of salvation?

Grant me a good end, grant me a happy passage out of this world.

Be mindful of me, O my God, and direct me in the right way to thy kingdom.   Amen.

CHAPTER 58

*That High Matters and God's Secret Judgments
Are Not to Be Narrowly Inquired Into*

My son beware thou dispute not of high matters nor of the hidden judgments of God, why this

---

[2]Gen. 3   [3]Psalm 119:103

man is forsaken, and that man taken into so great favor; why also this man is so much afflicted, and that man so greatly exalted.

These things are beyond the reach of man's understanding, neither is it in the power of any reason or disputation to search out the judgments of God.

When the Enemy therefore suggested these things unto thee, or some curious people raise the question, let thy answer be that of the Prophet, "Thou art just, O Lord, and thy judgment is right."[1]

And again, "The judgments of the Lord are true and righteous altogether."[2]

My judgments are to be feared, not to be discussed; for they can not be comprehended by the understanding of man.

2. In like manner I advise thee not to inquire, nor dispute of the merits of the saints, who among them is more holy than the other, or which is the greatest in the kingdom of heaven.

These things oftentimes breed strife and unprofitable contentions,[3] they also nourish pride and vain glory; from whence do spring envy and dissensions, whilst one will proudly prefer this, and the other another.

To desire to know and search out such things is to no purpose, nor would it please the saints; for I am not the God of dissension, but of peace; which peace consisteth rather in true humility, than in self-exaltation.

---

[1]Psalm 119:137   [2]Psalm 19:9   [3]2 Tim. 2:14

3. Some are carried with zeal of preference toward these or those saints; but this is rather human love than divine.

I am He who made all the saints; I gave them grace; I have obtained for them glory.

I know what every one hath deserved; I have prevented them with the blessings of my goodness.

I foreknew my beloved ones before the beginning of the world.

I chose them out of the world, they chose not me first.[4]

I called them by grace, I attracted them by mercy, I led them safe through sundry temptations.

I have poured into them glorious consolations, I have given them perseverance, I have crowned their patience.

4. I know both the first and the last; I embrace all with love inestimable.

I am to be praised in all my saints; I am to be blessed above all things, and to be honored in every one, whom I have thus gloriously exalted and predestinated without any precedent merits of their own.

He therefore that despiseth one of the least of my saints,[5] honoreth not the greatest; for that I made both the small and the great.[6]

And he that dispraiseth any of my saints, dispraiseth Me also, and all the rest in the kingdom of heaven.

---

[4]John 15:16   [5]James 2:1-5   [6]Wisd. 6:7

These all are one through the bond of love; they think the same, they will the same, and they all love one another.

5. Furthermore, which is a far higher consideration, they love Me more than they do themselves or any merits of their own.

For being rapt above self-love, they are wholly carried out to love Me, in whom also they rest with entire fruition.

Nothing can turn them back, nothing can press them down; for being full of the eternal Truth; they burn with the fire of unquenchable charity.

Let therefore carnal and natural men who can affect no other but their private joys, forbear to dispute of the state of the saints. They add and take away according to their own fancies, not as it pleaseth the eternal Truth.

6. Many are ignorant, especially those who are but little enlightened; and these can seldom love any with a perfect spiritual love.

They are as yet much drawn by a natural affection and human friendship to this man or to that; and according to the experience they have of themselves in their earthly affections, so they conceive imaginations of things heavenly.

But there is an incomparable distance between the things which the imperfect imagine in their conceits, and those which the illuminated are enabled to behold, through revelation from above.

7. Beware therefore, my son, that thou handle not with vain curiosity things which

exceed thy knowledge;[7] but rather so apply thy endeavors, that thou mayest at least have the lowest place in the kingdom of God.

Even if any one should know who exceeds another in sanctity, or who is accounted the greatest in the kingdom of heaven; what would this wisdom profit him, unless he should humble himself the more in my sight, and should rise up into the greater praising of my name, in proportion to this knowledge?

He pleaseth God much better that thinketh of the greatness of his sins, and the smallness of his graces, and how far off he is from the perfection of the saints, than he that disputeth of their greatness or littleness.

8. The saints are well, yea right well contented, if men would content themselves, and refrain from these their vain discourses.

They glory not of their own merits, for they ascribe no goodness to themselves, but attribute all to Me, who of my infinite love have given them all things.

They are filled with so great love of the Divinity, and with such an overflowing joy, that there is no glory nor happiness that is or can be wanting unto them.

All the saints, the higher they are in glory, so much the more humble are they in themselves, and the nearer and dearer unto Me.

And therefore thou hast it written, "That

---

[7]Ecclus. 3:21

they did cast their crowns before God, and fell down on their faces before the Lamb, and adored Him that Liveth for ever and ever."[8]

9. Many inquire, who is the greatest in the kingdom of God, that know not whether they shall ever be numbered there among the least.

It is a great thing to be even the least in heaven, where all are great; for that all these shall be called, and shall be, the Sons of God.

"The least shall become a thousand,"[9] and "the sinner of a hundred years shall die."[10]

For when the disciples asked who should be greatest in the kingdom of heaven, they received such an answer as this,

"Unless you be converted, and become as little children, you shall not enter into the kingdom of heaven; whosoever therefore shall humble himself as this little child, the same is the greatest in the kingdom of heaven."[11]

10. Woe be unto them who disdain to humble themselves willingly with little children; because the low gate of the kingdom of heaven will not give them entrance.[12]

Woe also to the rich, who have here their consolation; for while the poor enter into the kingdom of God, they shall stand lamenting outside.

Rejoice ye that be humble,[13] and ye poor be ye filled with joy, for yours is the kingdom of God, if at least you walk according to the Truth.

---

[8]Rev. 4:10   [9]Isaiah 60:22   [10]Isaiah 65:20
[11]Matt. 18:3   [12]Matt. 7:14   [13]Matt. 5:3

CHAPTER 59

That All Our Hope and Trust Is to Be Fixed in God Alone

Lord, what is my confidence which I have in this life? or what is the greatest comfort that all things under heaven do yield me?

It is not thou, O Lord my God, whose mercies are without number?

Where hath it ever been well with me without thee? or when could it be ill with me, when thou wert present?

I had rather be poor for thy sake, than rich without thee.

I rather choose to be a pilgrim on earth with thee, than without thee to possess heaven. Where thou art, there is heaven; and where thou art not, there is death and hell.

Thou art all my desire, and therefore I must needs sigh, and call, and earnestly pray unto thee.

In short, I have none fully to trust to, none that can seasonably help me in my necessities, but only thee, my God.

Thou art my trust, and my confidence, thou art my Comforter, and in all things most faithful unto me.

2. All men seek their own gain;[1] thou only settest forward my salvation and my profit, and turnest all things to my good.

---

[1] Phil. 2:21

Although thou exposest me to various temptations and adversities, yet thou orderest all this for my good, who art wont to prove thy beloved ones a thousand ways.

In which probation thou oughtest no less to be loved and praised; than if thou didst fill me full of heavenly consolations.

3. In thee, therefore, O Lord God, I place my whole hope and refuge; on thee I cast my tribulation and anguish; for I find all to be weak and inconstant, whatsoever I behold out of thee.

For many friends can not profit, nor strong helpers assist, nor prudent counsellors give a profitable answer, nor the books of the learned afford comfort, nor any precious substance deliver, nor any place, however retired and lovely, give shelter, unless thou thyself dost assist, help, strengthen, console, instruct, and guard us.

4. For all things that seem to belong to the attainment of peace and felicity, without thee, are nothing, and do bring in truth no felicity at all.

Thou therefore art the End of all that is good, the Height of life, the Depth of all that can be spoken; and to hope in thee above all things, is the strongest comfort of thy servants.

To thee therefore do I lift up mine eyes; in thee, my God, the Father of mercies, do I put my trust.

Bless and sanctify my soul with thy heavenly blessings, that it may become thy holy habitation, and the seat of thine eternal glory; and let nothing be found in this temple of thy dignity, which shall offend the eyes of thy Majesty.

According to the greatness of thy goodness and multitude of thy mercies, look upon me, and hear the prayer of thy poor servant, who is far exiled from thee, in the land of the shadow of death.

Protect and keep the soul of me, the meanest of thy servants, amid so many dangers of this corruptible life, and by thy grace accompanying me, direct it along the way of peace to its home of everlasting brightness. Amen.

THE FOURTH BOOK

Concerning the Sacrament

A Devout Exhortation to the Holy Communion

The voice of Christ.

"Come unto me, all ye that labor and are burdened, and I will refresh you,"[1] saith the Lord.

"The bread which I will give is my flesh, for the life of the world."[2]

"Take ye, and eat; this is my body, which is given for you:[3] do this in remembrance of me."[4]

"He that eateth my flesh and drinketh my blood dwelleth in me, and I in him."

"The words which I have spoken unto you are spirit and life."[5]

---

[1] Matt. 11:28   [2] John 6:51   [3] Matt. 26:26
[4] 1 Cor. 11:24   [5] John 6:56, 63

CHAPTER 1

With How Great Reverence Christ Ought to Be Received

The voice of the disciple.

These are thy words, O Christ, the everlasting Truth, though not spoken all at one time, nor written in one and the self-same place. Because therefore they are thine and true, they are all thankfully and faithfully to be received by me.

They are thine, and thou hast spoken them; and they are mine also, because thou hast spoken them for my salvation.

I cheerfully receive them from thy mouth, that they may be the more deeply implanted in my heart.

Those so gracious words, so full of sweetness and love, do encourage me; but mine own offences do dishearten me, and an impure conscience driveth me back from the receiving of so great mysteries.

The sweetness of thy words doth encourage me, but the multitude of my sins doth weigh me down.

2. Thou commandest me to come confidently unto thee, if I would have part with thee; and to receive the food of immortality, if I desire to obtain everlasting life and glory.

"Come unto me," sayest thou, "all ye that labor and are heavy laden, and I will refresh you."[1]

---

[1] Matt. 11:28

O sweet and loving word in the ear of a sinner, that thou, my Lord God, shouldest invite the poor and needy to the participation of thy most holy body!

But who am I, Lord, that I should presume to approach unto thee?

Behold, the heaven of heavens can not contain thee, and thou sayest, "Come ye all unto me."

3. What meaneth this so gracious a condescension, and this so loving invitation?

How shall I dare to come, who know not any good in myself, whereupon I may presume?

How shall I bring thee into my house, I that have so often offended thy most benign countenance?

Angels and archangels stand in awe of thee; saints and righteous men do fear thee, and sayest thou "Come ye all unto me?"

Unless thou, O Lord, didst say this, who would believe it to be true?

And unless thou didst command it, who could attempt to draw near [unto thee]?

Behold, Noah, a just man, labored a hundred years in the making of the ark,[2] that he might be saved with a few, and how can I in one hour's space prepare myself to receive with reverence the Maker of the world?

4. Moses, thy great servant, and thine especial friend, made an ark of incorruptible wood, which also he covered over with the finest gold, wherein to lay up the tables of the law;[3] and I, a

---

[2]Gen. 6:3   [3]Exodus 25:10-16

corrupted creature, how shall I dare so uncon-cernedly to receive the Maker of the law, and the Giver of life?

Solomon, the wisest of the kings of Israel, employed seven years in building a magnificent temple to the praise of thy name.[4]

He also celebrated the feast of dedication thereof eight days together; he offered a thou-sand peace-offerings, and he solemnly set the ark of the covenant in the place prepared for it, with the sound of trumpets, and great joy.[5]

And I, the most miserable and poorest of men, how shall I bring thee into my house, I that can scarce spend one half-hour in true devotion? And would that I could even once spend something like one half-hour in worthy and due manner!

5. O my God, how earnestly did they study and endeavor to please thee!

Alas, how little is that which I do! how short a time do I spend, when I am preparing myself to receive the communion!

Seldom am I wholly collected; very seldom indeed am I cleansed from all distraction.

And yet surely in the life-giving presence of thy Godhead, no unbecoming thought ought to intrude itself, nor should any creature occupy my heart; for I am about to entertain not an angel, but the Lord of angels.

6. And yet very great is the difference between the ark of the covenant with its relics,

---

[4]1 Kings 6:38   [5]1 Kings 8

and thy most pure body, with its unspeakable virtues; between those legal sacrifices, figures of things to come, and the true sacrifice of thy body, the fulfilment of all ancient sacrifices.

Why therefore am I not more ardent and zealous in seeking thine adorable presence?

Why do I not prepare myself with greater solicitude to receive thy holy things? whereas those holy ancient patriarchs and prophets, yea, kings also, and princes, with the whole people, showed such an affectionateness of devotion to thy divine service.

7. The most devout king David danced before the ark of God with all his might,[6] calling to mind the benefits bestowed in time past upon his forefathers. He made instruments of various kinds, he published psalms, and appointed them to be sung with joy; he also oftentimes himself sang to the harp, being inspired with the grace of the Holy Ghost. He taught the people of Israel to praise God with their whole hearts, and with voices full of harmony to bless and praise him every day.

If so great devotion was then displayed, and such celebrating of divine praise was kept up before the ark of the testament; what reverence and devotion ought now to be shown by me and all Christian people, during the ministration of the sacrament, in receiving the most precious body of Christ.

8. Many run to various places to visit the

---

[6] 2 Sam. 6:14

relics of the saints departed, are full of admiration at hearing of their deeds, behold with awe the spacious buildings of their temples, and kiss their sacred bones wrapped up in silk and gold.

But, behold, thou art thyself here present with me on thine altar, my God, Saint of saints, Creator of all things, and Lord of angels.

Often, in looking after such things, people are moved by curiosity, and the novelty of fresh sights, while little or no fruit of amendment is carried home; particularly when they go from place to place with such lightheartedness, without a true penitent heart.

But here, in this holy sacrament, thou art wholly present, my God, the man Christ Jesus: here, to all worthy and devout receivers, is granted an abundant fruit of eternal salvation.

There is here to attract men nothing that savors of levity, of curiosity, or of sensuality; nothing but firm faith, devout hope, and sincere charity.

9. O God, the invisible Creator of the world, how wonderfully dost thou deal with us! how sweetly and graciously dost thou dispose of all things with thine elect, to whom thou offerest thyself to be received in the sacrament.

For this verily exceedeth all understanding. This specially draweth the hearts of the devout, and inflameth their affections.

For even thy true faithful ones, who dispose their whole life to amendment, by this most precious sacrament, oftentimes gain much of the grace of devotion, and love of virtue.

10. Oh, the admirable and hidden grace of this sacrament, which only the faithful ones of Christ do know; but the unbelieving, and such as are slaves unto sin, can not have experience thereof!

In this sacrament spiritual grace is conferred, and strength which was lost is restored in the soul, and the beauty which by sin had been disfigured again returneth.

This grace is sometimes so great, that out of the fulness of devotion which is here given, not only the mind, but the weak body also, feeleth great increase of strength.

11. Nevertheless our coldness and negligence is much to be bewailed and pitied, that we are not drawn with greater affection to receive Christ, in whom all the hope of those that are to be saved doth consist, and all their merit.

For he himself is our sanctification and redemption; he himself is the comfort of those who are here but travellers, and the everlasting fruition of saints.

It is therefore much to be lamented that many do so little consider this saving mystery, which causeth joy in heaven, and preserveth the whole world.

Alas for the blindness and hardness of man's heart, that doth not more deeply weigh so unspeakable a gift; but rather cometh by the daily use thereof to regard it little or nothing!

12. For if this most holy sacrament were to be celebrated in one place only, and consecrated

by one only priest in the world, with how great desires dost thou think would men be affected to that place, and toward such a priest of God, that they might be witnesses of the celebration of these divine mysteries?

But now many are made priests, and in many places Christ is offered; that the grace and love of God to man may appear so much the greater, the more widely this sacred communion is spread over the world.

Thanks be unto thee, O merciful Jesu, thou eternal Shepherd, that thou hast consented to refresh us, who are poor, and in a state of banishment, with thy precious body and blood, to invite us to the receiving of these Mysteries with the words even of thine own mouth, saying, "Come unto Me all ye that labor and are heavy laden, and I will refresh you."

CHAPTER 2

That the Great Goodness and Love of God Is Exhibited to Man in This Sacrament

The voice of the disciple.

In confidence of thy goodness and great mercy, O Lord, I draw near, as a sick person to the Healer, as one hungry and thirsty to the Fountain of life, a needy wretch to the King of heaven, a servant unto his Lord, a creature to the

Creator, a desolate soul to my own tender Comforter.

But whence is this to me, that thou hast consented to come unto me?[1] what am I, that thou shouldst give thine own self unto me?

How dare a sinner appear before thee? and how is it that thou dost consent to come unto a sinner?

Thou knowest thy servant, thou seest that he hath in him no good thing, for which thou shouldest bestow this favor upon him.

I confess therefore mine own unworthiness, I acknowledge thy goodness, I praise thy tender mercy and give thee thanks for this thy transcendent love.

For thou dost this for thine own sake, not for any merits of mine; to the end that thy goodness may be better known unto me, thy love more abundantly poured down, and thy gracious humility the more eminently set forth.

Since therefore it is thy pleasure, and thou hast commanded that it should be so, this thy condescension is also dearly pleasing unto me, and oh, that my iniquity may be no hinderance herein!

2. O most sweet and most benign Jesu, how great reverence and thanksgiving, together with perpetual praise, is due unto thee for the receiving of thy sacred body, whose preciousness no mortal man is able to express.

---

[1]Luke 1:43

But on what shall I think at this Communion, in making this approach unto my Lord, whom I am not able duly to honor, and yet whom I can not but desire devoutly to receive?

What can I think on better, and more profitable, than utterly to humble myself before thee, and to exalt thine infinite goodness above me:

I praise thee, my God, and will exalt thee for ever; I do despise myself, and cast myself down before thee, into the depth of mine own unworthiness.

Behold, thou art the Holy of Holies, and I the scum of sinners!

Behold, thou inclinest thyself unto me, who am not worthy so much as to look up unto thee!

Behold, thou comest unto me; it is thy will to be with me; thou invitest me to thy banquet.

Thou art willing to give me heavenly food and bread of angels to eat,[2] which is indeed no other than thyself the Living Bread, which camest down from heaven and givest life unto the world.

4. Behold, from whence doth this love proceed! what a gracious condescension of thine shineth forth! how great thanks and praises are due unto thee for these benefits!

O how good and profitable was thy counsel, when thou didst ordain it! how sweet and pleasant the banquet, when thou gavest thyself to be our food!

---

[2]Psalm 78:25; John 6:33

O how wonderful is this thy doing, O Lord, how mighty is thy power, how unspeakable thy truth!

For thou didst speak the word and all things were made;[3] and this was done which thou thyself commandedst.

5. A matter of great admiration, worthy of all faith, and surpassing man's understanding, that thou my Lord God, true God and man, shouldst offer thyself wholly to us in a little bread and wine, and therein become our inexhaustible support.

Thou who art the Lord of all things, and standest in need of none,[4] art pleased to dwell in us by means of this thy sacrament.

Do thou preserve my heart and body unspotted, that with a cheerful and pure conscience I may be able often to celebrate, and to receive to my everlasting health, those mysteries, which thou didst specially ordain and institute for thine own honor, and for a never-ceasing memorial of thyself.

6. Rejoice, O my soul, and give thanks unto God, for so noble a gift, and so precious a consolation, left unto thee in this vale of tears.

For as often as thou callest to mind this mystery, and receivest the body of Christ, so often dost thou go over the work of thy redemption, and art made partaker of all the merits of Christ.

For the love of Christ is never diminished,

[3]Gen. 1; Psalm 148:5   [4]Psalm 16:2

and the greatness of his propitiation is never exhausted.

Therefore thou oughtest to dispose thyself hereto by a constant fresh renewing of thy mind, and to weigh with attentive consideration this great mystery of thy salvation.

So great, so new, and so joyful ought it to seem unto thee, when thou celebratest or partakest in these holy mysteries, as if on this same day Christ first descending into the womb of the Virgin, was made man, or was hanging on the cross, did this day suffer and die for the salvation of mankind.

CHAPTER 3

That It Is Profitable to Communicate Often

The voice of the disciple.

Behold, O Lord, I come unto thee, that I may be comforted in thy gift, and be delighted in thy holy banquet, which thou, O God, hast in thy goodness prepared for the poor.[1]

Behold in thee is all whatsoever I can or ought to desire; and thou art my salvation and my redemption, my hope and my strength, my honor and glory.

Make joyful therefore this day the soul of thy

---

[1] Psalm 68:10

servant;[2] for unto thee, O Lord Jesu, have I lifted up my soul.

I desire to receive thee now with devotion and reverence. I do long to bring thee into my house, that with Zaccheus I may deserve to be blessed by thee, and to be numbered amongst the children of Abraham.

My soul longeth to receive thy body, my heart desireth to be united with thee.

2. Give thyself to me, and it sufficeth; for without thee no comfort is available.

Without thee I can not be, nor endure to live without thy visitation.

And therefore I must needs often draw near unto thee, and receive thee for the welfare of my soul; lest perhaps I faint in the way, if I be deprived of the heavenly food.

For so, most merciful Jesus, thou once didst say, preaching to the people and curing various diseases, "I will not send them home fasting, lest they faint in the way."[3]

Deal thou therefore in like manner now with me, who hast agreed to leave thyself in the sacrament for the comfort of the faithful.

For thou art the sweet refection of the soul; and he that eateth thee worthily, shall be partaker and heir of everlasting glory.

It is necessary for me, who so often fall into error and sin, who so quickly grow dull and faint, that by frequent prayer and confession,

---

[2]Psalm 86:4   [3]Matt. 15:32; Mark 8:3

and receiving of thy holy body, I may renew, cleanse, and inflame myself, lest perhaps by long abstaining, I should fall away from my holy purposes.

3. For the imaginations of man are prone unto evil from his youth,[4] and unless some divine remedy help him, he quickly falleth to worse.

This holy communion therefore draweth back from evil and strengtheneth in good.

For if I be now so often negligent and cold when I communicate, or celebrate; what would become of me if I received not this remedy, and sought not after so great a help?

Although every day I be not fit, nor well prepared to communicate; I will endeavor notwithstanding at due times to receive the divine mysteries, and to be partaker of so great a grace.

For this is one chief consolation of faithful souls, so long as they are absent from thee in this mortal body, that being often mindful of their God, they receive their beloved with a devout mind.

4. O the wonderful condescension of thy tender mercy toward us, that thou O Lord God, the Creator and Giver of life to all spirit, dost consent to come unto a poor soul, and with thy whole Deity and humanity to replenish the hunger thereof!

O happy minds and blessed souls, who have

---

[4]Gen. 8:21

the privilege of receiving thee, their Lord God, with devout affection, and in so receiving thee, are permitted to be full of spiritual joy!

O, how great a Lord do they entertain! How beloved a Guest do they harbor! How delightful a Companion do they receive! How faithful a Friend do they welcome! How lovely and noble a Companion do they embrace! even him who is to be loved above all that are beloved, and above all things that can be desired.

O thou, the most sweet, most beloved, let heaven and earth, and all their ornaments, be silent in thy presence; for what praise and beauty soever they have, it is received from thy bounteous condescension, and shall never equal the grace and beauty of thy name, whose wisdom is beyond all numbers.[5]

CHAPTER 4

*That Many Benefits Are Bestowed Upon Them
That Communicate Devoutly*

The voice of the disciple.

O Lord, my God, do thou present thy servant with blessings of thy sweetness,[1] that I may approach worthily and devoutly to thy glorious sacrament.

---

[5]Psalm 147:5   [1]Psalm 21:3

Stir up my heart unto thee, and deliver me from all dulness; visit me with thy salvation,[2] that I may taste in spirit thy sweetness, which plentifully lieth hid in this sacrament as in a fountain.

Enlighten also mine eyes to behold so great a mystery, and strengthen me with undoubting faith to believe it.

For it is thy work, and no human power; thy sacred institution, not man's invention.

For of himself no man is able to comprehend and understand these things, which transcend even the exquisite skill of angels.

What portion, then, of so high and sacred a mystery shall I, unworthy sinner, dust and ashes, be able to search out and comprehend?

2. O Lord, in the simplicity of my heart, with a good and firm faith, and at thy commandment, I draw near unto thee with hope and reverence; and I do truly believe that thou art here present in this sacrament, both God and man.

Thy will is that I should receive thee, and that I should unite myself unto thee in charity.

Wherefore I implore thy mercy, and do crave thy special grace, to the end I may wholly be dissolved and overflow with love unto thee, and hereafter never suffer any external consolation to enter in.

For this most high and precious sacrament is

---

[2]Psalm 106:4

the health both of soul and body, the medicine for all spiritual languor; hereby my vices are cured, my passions bridled, my temptations overcome, or at least weakened; greater grace is infused, virtue begun is increased, faith is confirmed, hope strengthened, and love inflamed and enlarged.

3. For thou hast bestowed, and still oftentimes dost bestow many benefits in this sacrament upon thy beloved ones that communicate devoutly, O my God, the protector of my soul, the Strengthener of human frailty, and the Giver of all inward comfort.

Thou impartest unto them much comfort against many tribulations; and liftest them up from the depth of their own dejected state, to hope in thy protection; and dost inwardly recreate and enlighten them with new grace, so that they who at first, and before communion, felt themselves full of anxiety and heartlessness, afterward being refreshed with heavenly meat and drink, do find in themselves a change for the better.

And in such a way of dispensation thou dealest with thine elect, that they may truly acknowledge, and clearly acknowledge, how great their own infirmity is, and what goodness and grace they obtain from thee.

For they of themselves are cold, dull, and undevout, but by thee they are made fervent, cheerful, and full of devotion.

For who is there, that, approaching humbly

unto the fountain of sweetness, doth not carry away thence at least some little sweetness?

Or who standing by a great fire, receiveth not some small heat thereby?

And thou art a fountain always full and overflowing, a fire ever burning and never decaying.[3]

4. Wherefore, if I am not permitted to draw out of the full fountain itself, nor to drink my fill, I will, notwithstanding, set my lips to the mouth of this heavenly conduit, that I may receive thence at least some small drop to refresh my thirst, that so I may not be wholly dried up.

As though I can not as yet be altogether heavenly, nor so inflamed as the cherubim and seraphim, yet notwithstanding I will endeavor to apply myself earnestly to devotion, and prepare my heart to obtain if it be but some small spark of divine fire, by the humble receiving of this life-giving sacrament.

And whatsoever is hereunto wanting in me, O merciful Jesus, most Holy Savior, do thou bountifully and graciously supply for me, thou who hast agreed to call us all unto thee, saying, "Come unto me all ye that labor and are burdened, and I will refresh you."[4]

5. I indeed labor in the sweat of my brow,[5] I am vexed with grief of heart, I am burdened with sins, I am troubled with temptations, I am entangled and oppressed with many evil pas-

---

[3] Isaiah 12:3; Lev. 6:13 [4] Matt. 11:28 [5] Gen. 3:19

sions; and there is none to help me, none to deliver and save me, but thou, O Lord God my Savior, to whom I commit myself, and all that is mine, that thou mayest keep watch over me, and bring me safe to life everlasting.

Receive me for the honor and glory of thy name, thou who hast prepared thy body and blood to be my meat and drink.

Grant, O Lord God, my Savior, that by frequenting thy mysteries, the zeal of my devotion may grow and increase.

CHAPTER 5

Of the Dignity of the Sacrament, and of the Ministerial Function

The voice of the Beloved.

If thou hadst angelical purity[1] and the sanctity of St. John Baptist, thou wouldst not be worthy either to receive or to administer this sacrament.

For it is not within the compass of the merits of men, that man should consecrate and administer the sacrament of Christ, and receive for food the bread of angels.[2]

Grand is this mystery; and great is the dignity of the priests, to whom is granted that which is not permitted to angels.

---

[1]Matt. 18:10   [2]Psalm 78:25

For none but priests rightly ordained in the church, have power to celebrate this sacrament and to consecrate the body of Christ.

The priest is indeed the minister of God, using the word of God by God's command and appointment: but God is there the principal Author, and invisible Worker; to whom is subject all that he shall please, and all that he commandeth doth obey.[3]

2. Thou oughtest therefore more to believe God Almighty in this most excellent sacrament, than thine own sense, or any visible sign.

And therefore thou art to approach this holy work with fear and reverence.

Consider attentively with thyself,[4] and see what that is, whereof the ministry is delivered unto thee by the laying on of the bishop's hand.

Behold, thou art made a priest, and consecrated to celebrate the Lord's sacraments; take heed now that thou offer the Christian sacrifice to God faithfully and devoutly, and at fit opportunities, and conduct thyself so, as thou mayest be without reproof.

Thou hast not lightened thy burden, but art now bound with a straighter band of discipline, and art obliged to a more perfect degree of sanctity.

A priest ought to be adorned with all graces, and to give example of a good life to others.

His life and conversation[5] should not be in

---

[3]Gen. 1; Psalm 49:7; Rom. 9:20
[4]1 Tim. 4:16   [5]Phil. 3:20

the popular and common ways of men, but with the angels in heaven, or with perfect men on earth.

3. A priest clad in sacred garments is Christ's deputy, that with all supplication and humility he may beseech God for himself and for the whole people.[6]

Neither ought he to cease from prayer and holy oblation, till he prevail to obtain grace and mercy.

When a priest doth celebrate the holy eucharist, he honoreth God, he rejoiceth the angels, he edifieth the church, he helpeth the living, and he commemorateth the departed, and maketh himself partaker of all good things.

CHAPTER 6

An Inquiry Concerning Spiritual Exercise Before Communion

The voice of the disciple.

When I weigh thy worthiness, O Lord, and mine own vileness, I tremble exceedingly, and am confounded within myself.

For if I come not unto thee, I fly from life, and if I unworthily intrude myself, I incur thy displeasure.

---

[6]Heb. 5:3

What therefore shall I do, O my God, my Helper and my Counsellor in all necessity?

2. Teach thou me the right way, appoint me some brief exercise, suitable to this holy communion.

For it is good for me to know how I should reverently and religiously prepare my heart for thee, for the profitable receiving of thy sacrament, or for the celebrating of so great and divine a sacrifice.

CHAPTER 7

*Of Thoroughly Examining Our Own Conscience,
and of Holy Purposes of Amendment*

The voice of the Beloved.

Above all things, God's priest ought to come to celebrate, and to receive this sacrament with very great humility of heart, and with reverential supplication, with a full faith, and a dutiful regard for God's honor.

Examine diligently thy conscience, and to the utmost of thy power purify and cleanse it with true contrition and humble confession; so that there may be nothing in thee that may be burdensome unto thee, or that may breed in thee remorse of conscience, and hinder thy free access to the throne of grace.

Be grieved at the recollection of all thy sins in general, and in particular bewail and lament thy daily transgressions.

And if thou hast time, confess unto God in the secret of thine heart all the miserable evils of thy disordered passions.

2. Lament thou, and grieve, that thou art yet so carnal and worldly, so unmortified in thy passions, so full of the motions of concupiscence:

So unwatchful over thy outward senses, so often entangled with many vain fancies:

So much inclined to outward things, so negligent in the interior:

So prone to laughter and immodesty, so indisposed to tears and compunction:

So prompt to ease and pleasures of the flesh, so dull to strictness of life and zeal:

So curious to hear news, and see glorious sights, so slack to embrace what is humble and low:

So covetous of abundance, so sparing in giving, so close in keeping:

So inconsiderate in speech, so unbridled to silence:

So uncomposed in manners, so fretful in action:

So immoderate in food, so deaf to the word of God:

So hasty to rest, so slow to labor:

So wakeful to hear gossiping tales, so drowsy at the sacred services:

So hasty to arrive at the end thereof, so inclined to be wandering and inattentive:

So negligent in the prayers, so lukewarm in celebrating the holy eucharist, so dry and heartless in receiving it:

So quickly distracted, so seldom wholly gathered into thyself:

So suddenly moved to anger, so apt to take displeasure against another:

So ready to judge, so severe to reprove:

So joyful in prosperity, so weak in adversity:

So often making many good resolutions, and yet bringing them at last to so poor effect.

3. These and other of thy defects being confessed and bewailed with sorrow, and great displeasure at thine own infirmity, make thou a firm resolution always to be amending thy life, and to be endeavoring still after a further progress in holiness.

Then, with full resignation and with thy whole will, do thou to the honor of my name, offer up thyself a perpetual whole burnt-offering on the altar of thy heart, faithfully committing thy body and soul unto me.

And then thou mayest be accounted worthy to draw near to celebrate this sacrifice unto God, and to receive profitably the sacrament of my body.

4. For man hath no oblation more worthy, nor any greater for the washing away of sin, than to offer himself unto God purely and wholly, in the holy communion of the body and blood of Christ.

And when a man shall have done what lieth in him, and shall be truly penitent, as often as he shall come to Me for pardon and grace, "As I live," saith the Lord, "who will not the death of a sinner, but rather that he be converted and live,[1] I will not remember his sins any more, but they shall all be forgiven him."

CHAPTER 8

Of the Offering of Christ on the Cross, and of Resignation of Ourselves

The voice of the Beloved.

Of my own will did I offer up Myself unto God the Father for thy sins,[1] my hands being stretched forth on the cross, and my body laid bare, so that nothing remained in Me that was not wholly turned into a sacrifice for the appeasing of the divine Majesty.

In like manner oughtest thou also to offer thyself willingly unto Me every day in the holy communion, as a pure and sacred oblation, with all thy strength and affections, and to the utmost stretch of thine inward faculties.

What do I require of thee more, than that thou study to resign thyself entirely unto Me?

Whatsoever thou givest beside thyself, is of

[1]Ezek. 18:22-23   [1]Isaiah 53:5; Heb. 9:28

no value in my sight, for I seek not thy gifts, but thee.[2]

2. As it would not suffice thee to have all things whatsoever, beside Me; so neither can it please Me, whatever thou givest, if thou offer not thyself.

Offer up thyself unto Me, and give thyself wholly for God, and thy offering shall be acceptable.

Behold, I offered up Myself wholly unto my Father for thee, and gave my whole body and blood for thy food, that I might be wholly thine, and that thou mightest continue mine to the end.

But if thou abidest in thyself, and dost not offer thyself up freely unto my will, thy offering is not entire, neither will there be perfect union between us.

Therefore a free offering up of thyself into the hands of God ought to go before all thine actions, if thou desire to obtain liberty and grace.

For this cause so few become inwardly free and illuminated, because they are loath wholly to deny themselves.

My sentence standeth sure, "Unless a man forsake all, he can not be my disciple."[3] If thou therefore desire to be my disciple, offer up thyself unto Me with thy whole affections.

---

[2]Prov. 23:26   [3]Luke 14:33

CHAPTER 9

That We Ought to Offer Up Ourselves, and All
That Is Ours, Unto God, and to Pray for All

The voice of the disciple.

Thine, O Lord, are all things that are in heaven, and in earth.[1]

I desire to offer up myself unto thee, as a free offering and to continue thine for ever.

O Lord, in the simplicity of my heart I offer myself unto thee this day, in humble submission, for a sacrifice of a perpetual praise, and to be thy servant for ever.

Receive thou me, with this holy offering of thy precious body; which I make to thee this day in the presence of angels invisibly attending; and may this be for my good and the good of all thy people.

2. I offer unto thee, O Lord, all my sins and offences, which I have committed before thee, and thy holy angels, from the day wherein I first could sin, to this hour, upon thy merciful altar, that thou mayest consume and burn them all with the fire of thy love, and wash out all the stains of my sins, and cleanse my conscience from all offences, and restore to me again thy grace which I lost by sin, forgiving me all my

---

[1]Psalm 24:1

offences, and receiving me mercifully to the kiss of peace.

3. What can I do with my sins,[2] but humbly confess and bewail them, and entreat always thy favor and propitiation?

I beseech thee, hear me graciously, when I stand before thee, my God.

All my sins are very displeasing unto me, I will never commit them any more; but for them I do grieve, and will grieve as long as I live, and am resolved to repent and according to the utmost of my power to make restitution.

Forgive me, O God, forgive me my sins for the sake of thy holy name, save thou my soul which thou hast redeemed with thy most precious blood.

Behold I commit myself unto thy mercy, I resign myself into thy hands.

Deal with me according to thy goodness, not according to my wickedness and iniquity.

4. I offer up also unto thee all of what is good in me, although it be very small and imperfect, that thou mayest amend and sanctify it, that thou mayest make it grateful and acceptable unto thee, and always perfect it more and more; and bring me also, who am a slothful and unprofitable poor creature, to a good and blessed end.

5. I offer up also unto thee all the pious

---

[2]Psalm 32:5

desires of devout persons, the necessities of parents, friends, brethren, sisters, and of all those that are dear unto me, and that have done good either to myself or to others for thy love.

Also I commend unto thee, all that have desired and begged of me to pray for them and all theirs, whether they still live in the flesh, or have departed this life.

Grant that all may receive the help of thy grace, the aid of thy consolation, protection from dangers, deliverance from pain; and that being freed from all evils, they may with joy return abundant thanksgivings unto thee.

6. I offer up also unto thee my prayers and intercessions for those especially who have in anything wronged, grieved, or slandered me, or have done me any hurt or injury.

I pray for all those also, whom I have at any time vexed, troubled, grieved, and scandalized by words or deeds, knowingly or in ignorance; that it may please thee to forgive us all our sins and offences, one against another.

Take away from our hearts, O Lord, all suspiciousness, indignation, wrath, and contention, and whatsoever may hurt charity, and lessen brotherly love.

Have mercy, O Lord, have mercy on those that crave thy mercy, give grace unto them that stand in need thereof, and make us such as that we may be counted worthy to enjoy thy grace and go forward to life eternal.   Amen.

CHAPTER 10

That the Holy Communion Is Not Lightly to Be Forborne

The voice of the beloved.

Thou oughtest often to have recourse to the fountain of grace and of divine mercy, to the fountain of goodness and of all purity; that thou mayest be healed of thy sins and passions, and be made more strong and vigilant against all the temptations and deceits of the devil.

The enemy knowing what exceeding great profit and restorative aid comes by the holy communion, endeavoreth by all means and occasions to withdraw and hinder faithful and devout persons from partaking therein.

2. Thus it is that some persons when they are preparing to fit themselves for holy communion, suffer from the illusions of Satan worse than before.

That wicked spirit himself cometh amongst the sons of God,[1] to trouble them according to his accustomed malice, or to render them over fearful and perplexed; that so he may diminish their affections, or by direct assaults take away their faith, to the end he may prevail on them if possible either altogether to forbear communicating, or at least to come with lukewarmness.

---

[1] Job. 1:6

But there is no heed at all to be taken of these his crafty and fanciful suggestions, be they never so shameful and hideous, but all such vain imaginations are to be turned back upon his own head.

Thou must despise and laugh to scorn the miserable wretch, nor dare to omit the holy communion on account of his assaults, or for the troubles which he awakens within thee.

3. Oftentimes also an over-great solicitude for the obtaining a certain degree of devotion, and a kind of anxiety about the confession of sins hindereth thee.

Follow herein the counsel of the wise[2] and lay aside all anxiety and scrupulousness for it hinders the grace of God, and overthrows the devotion of the mind.

Do not omit the holy communion for every trifling vexation and trouble, but rather proceed at once to confess thy sins, and cheerfully forgive others whatever offences they have done against thee;

And if thou hast offended anyone, humbly crave pardon, and God will readily forgive thee.[3]

4. What availeth it to delay long the confession of thy sins, or to defer the holy communion?

Make thyself thoroughly clean as soon as possible, spit out the poison with all speed,

[2]Prov. 13   [3]Matt. 6:14

make haste to apply this sovereign remedy, and thou shalt find it to be better with thee, than if thou long defer it.

If thou omit it today for one cause, perhaps tomorrow another of greater force may occur to thee; and so thou mayest be hindered a long time from communion, and grow more and more unfit.

As quickly as ever thou canst, shake off from thyself all present heaviness and sloth, for it is of no use to continue long in uneasiness, or to be going on long with a disturbed conscience, and so for everyday impediments to withdraw thyself from divine service.

Yea, it is very hurtful to defer the communion long, for this usually brings on a heavy spiritual drowsiness.

Alas, some lukewarm undisciplined persons do willingly delay confession, and defer the holy communion, lest they should be obliged to keep a stricter watch over themselves.

5. Oh, how poor and mean is their love, how weak their devotion, who so easily put off the holy communion!

How happy is he and how acceptable to God, who so ordereth his life, and in such purity keepeth his conscience, that he is prepared and well-disposed to communicate even every day, if it were in his power, and might be done without others taking notice.

If a person do sometimes abstain out of humility, or by reason of some lawful cause preventing him, he is to be commended so far as he shows a feeling of reverence.

But if a spiritual drowsiness have crept over him, he must stir himself up, and do what lieth in him, and the Lord will assist his desire, for the goodwill he hath thereto, which is what God doth chiefly respect.

6. But when any lawful hinderance doth happen, he will yet always have a goodwill, and a pious intention to communicate, and so shall he not lose the fruit of the sacrament.

For any devout person may every day and every hour profitably and without prohibition draw near to Christ in spiritual communion.

And yet on certain days, and at time appointed, he ought to receive sacramentally, with affectionate reverence, the body of his Redeemer, and rather seek the honor and glory of God, than his own comfort.[4]

For he communicateth mystically, and is invisibly refreshed, as often as he devoutly calleth to mind the mystery of the incarnation and the passion of Christ, and is inflamed with the love of him.

7. He that prepareth not himself, except only when a festival draweth near, or when custom compelleth him thereunto, shall too often be unprepared.

Blessed is he that offereth himself up as a

---

[4] 1 Cor. 11

whole burnt offering to the Lord, as often as he doth administer or receive the holy communion.

Be not too long nor too short in celebrating the mystical service, but keep the good-accustomed manner of those with whom thou livest.

Thou oughtest not to be tedious and troublesome to others, but to observe the received custom, according to the appointment of our fathers, and rather to yield thyself up to the profit of others, than to thine own devotion or feelings.

CHAPTER 11

That the Body of Christ and the Holy Scriptures Are Most Necessary Unto a Faithful Soul

The voice of the disciple.

O blessed Lord Jesus, how great is the blessedness of a devout soul that feasteth with thee in thy banquet, where there is set no other food to be eaten but thyself, the only beloved, and most to be desired above all the desires of the heart!

And verily it should be a sweet thing unto me to pour out tears from the very bottom of my heart in thy presence, and with loving Magdalene to wash thy feet with my tears.[1]

---

[1] Luke 7:38

But where now is that devotion? where that plentiful effusion of holy tears?

Surely in thy sight and thy holy angels, my whole heart should be inflamed, and even weep for joy.

For in the sacrament I have thee truly present, though hidden under another representation.

2. For to behold thee in thine own, thy divine brightness, mine eyes would not be able to endure, nor could even the whole world stand in the splendor of the glory of thy Majesty.

Herein then dost thou have regard to my weakness, that thou dost conceal thyself under this outward sacramental sign.

Him I do really possess and adore, whom the angels adore in heaven; but I, for the present and in the meantime, by faith, they by sight, and without a veil.

I must be content with the light of true faith, and to walk therein, until the day of everlasting brightness shall dawn, and the shadows of figures pass away.

But when that which is perfect is come, the use of sacraments shall cease;[2] because the blessed in heavenly glory need not any sacramental remedy.

For they rejoice without end in the presence of God, beholding his glory face to face; and being transformed from glory to glory into the image of the incomprehensible Deity, they taste

---

[2] 1 Cor. 42:10

the Word of God made flesh, as he was from the beginning, and as he abideth for ever.

3. While I am mindful of these wonderful things, even all spiritual comfort whatsoever becometh tedious unto me; because as long as I behold not my Lord openly in his own glory, I make no account at all of whatsoever I see or hear in this world.

Thou art my witness, O God, that nothing can comfort me, no creature can give me rest, but thou my God, whom I long to contemplate everlastingly.

But this is not possible so long as I linger in this mortality.

Therefore I must frame myself to much patience; and submit myself to thee in all my desires.

For even thy saints, O Lord, who now rejoice with thee in the kingdom of heaven, while they lived, waited in faith and in great patience for the coming of thy glory.[3] What they believed, I believe also; what they hoped for, I hope for; whither they are arrived, I trust I shall come by thy grace.

In the meantime I will walk in faith, strengthened by the examples of the saints.

I have also holy books for my comfort and for the glass of my life, and above all these, [I have] thy most holy body for a singular remedy and refuge.

---

[3]Heb. 10:35-36; 11

4. For I perceive two things to be very particularly necessary for me in this life, without which this miserable life would be unsupportable unto me.

While I am detained in the prison of this body, I acknowledge myself to stand in need of two things, namely, food and light.

Unto me then thus weak and helpless thou hast given thy sacred body, for the refreshment both of my soul and body;[4] and thy word thou hast set as a light unto my feet.[5]

Without these two I should not well be able to live; for the word of God is the light of my soul, and thy sacrament the bread of life.

These also may be called the two tables, set on the one side and on the other, in the treasury and jewel-house of the holy church.[6]

One table is that of the sacred altar, having the holy bread, that is, the precious body of Christ; the other is that of divine law, containing holy doctrine, teaching men the right faith, and strongly conducting them forward even to that within the veil, where is the holy of holies.

Thanks be unto thee, O Lord Jesus, thou Light of everlasting Light, for that table of holy doctrine which thou hast prepared for us by thy servants the prophets, and apostles, and other teachers.

---

[4]John 6:51   [5]Psalm 119:105
[6]Psalm 23:5; Heb. 9:2; 8:10

[309]

5. Thanks be unto thee, O thou Creator and Redeemer of mankind, who, to manifest thy love to the whole world, hast prepared a great supper,[7] wherein thou hast set before us to be eaten, not the typical lamb, but thine own most sacred body and blood,[8] rejoicing all the faithful with this holy banquet, and replenishing them to the full with the cup of salvation,[9] in which are all the delights of Paradise; and the holy angels do feast with us, but yet with a more happy sweetness.

6. Oh, how great and honorable is the office of God's priests, to whom it is given with sacred words to consecrate the sacrament of the Lord of Glory, with their lips to bless, with their hands to hold, with their own mouth to receive, and also to administer to others!

Oh, how clean ought those hands to be, how pure that mouth, how holy that body, how unspotted that heart, where the Author of purity so often entereth!

Nothing but what is holy, no word but what is good and profitable, ought to proceed from his mouth, who so often receiveth the sacrament of Christ.

7. Simple and chaste ought to be the eyes that are accustomed to behold the body of Christ; the hands should be pure and lifted up to heaven, that are used to touch the Creator of heaven and earth.

---

[7]Luke 14:16   [8]John 6:53-56
[9]Psalm 23:5; Wisd. 16:20-21

Unto the priests especially it is said in the law, "Be ye holy, for that I the Lord your God am holy."[10]

8. O Almighty God, do thou assist us with thy grace, that we who have undertaken the office of the priesthood, may be able to serve thee worthily and devoutly, in all purity, and with a good conscience.

And if we live not in so great innocence as we ought to do, grant to us at the least worthily to lament the sins which we have committed; and in the spirit of humility, and with the full purpose of a good will, to serve thee more earnestly for the time to come.

CHAPTER 12

That He Who Is About to Communicate With Christ Ought to Prepare Himself With Great Diligence

The voice of the Beloved.

I am the Lover of purity, and the Giver of all sanctity.

I seek a pure heart, and there is the place of my rest.[1]

Make ready for Me a large upper room furnished,[2] and I will keep the passover at thy house with my disciples.

If thou wilt have me come unto thee, and

---

[10]Lev. 19:2; 20:26   [1]Psalm 24:4; Matt. 5:8
[2]Mark 14:14-15; Luke 22:11-12

remain with thee; purge out the old leaven,[3] and make clean the habitation of thy heart.

Shut out the whole world,[4] and all the throng of sins; sit thou as it were a sparrow alone upon the house-top, and think over thy transgressions in the bitterness of thy soul.

For every one that loveth will prepare the best and fairest place for his beloved; for herein is known the affection of him that entertaineth his beloved.

2. Know thou notwithstanding, that the merit of no action of thine is able to make this preparation sufficient, although thou shouldest prepare thyself a whole year together, and have nothing else on thy mind.

But it is out of my mere grace and favor that thou art permitted to come to my table, as if a beggar were invited to a rich man's dinner; and he hath no other return to make to him for his benefits, but to humble himself and give him thanks.

Do what lieth in thee, and do it diligently; not for custom, not for necessity; but with fear and reverence, and affection, receive the body of thy beloved Lord God, when he consents to come unto thee.

I am He that have called thee, I have commanded it to be done, I will supply what is wanting in thee; come thou and receive me.

3. When I bestow on thee the grace of

---

[3]1 Cor. 5:7   [4]Exodus 24:18

devotion, give thanks to thy God; for it is given thee, not because thou art worthy, but because I have had mercy on thee.

If thou have it not, but rather dost feel thyself dry, be instant in prayer, sigh, and knock, and give not over until thou art meet to receive some crumb or drop of saving grace.

Thou hast need of me, I have no need of thee.

Neither comest thou to sanctify me, but I come to sanctify and make thee better.

Thou comest that thou mayest be sanctified by me, and united unto me, that thou mayest receive new grace, and be stirred up anew to amendment of life.

Neglect not this grace, but prepare thy heart with all diligence, and receive thy beloved into thy soul.

4. But thou oughtest not only to prepare thyself to devotion before communion, but carefully also to preserve thyself therein, after thou hast received the sacrament.

Nor is the careful guard of thyself afterward less required, than devout preparation before.

For a good guard afterward is the best preparation again for the obtaining of greater grace.

For if a person gives himself up at once too much to outward consolations, he is rendered thereby greatly indisposed to devotion.

Beware of much talk,[5] remain in some secret

---

[5] Prov. 10:19

place, and enjoy thy God; for thou hast him, whom all the world can not take from thee.

I am He, to whom thou oughtest wholly to give up thyself, that so thou mayest now live the rest of thy time, not in thyself, but in me, free from all anxiety.

CHAPTER 13

That the Devout Soul Ought With the Whole Heart to Seek Communion With Christ in the Sacrament

The voice of the disciple.

How shall I obtain this favor, O Lord, to find thee alone and by thyself, open unto thee my whole heart, and to enjoy thee even as my soul desireth? so that henceforth none may look upon me, nor any creature move me, or have regard to me, but that thou alone mayest speak unto me, and I to thee, as the beloved is wont to speak to his beloved, and a friend to banquet with his friend.[1]

This I beg, this I long for, that I may be wholly united unto thee, and may withdraw my heart from all created things, and may learn more and more by means of sacred communion and the often celebrating thereof, to relish things heavenly and eternal.

[1]Exodus 33:11; Canticles 8:2

Ah, Lord God, when shall I be wholly united to thee, and absorbed by thee, and become altogether forgetful of myself?

"Thou in me, and I in thee,"[2] so also grant that we may both continue together in one.

2. Verily, thou art my beloved, the choicest amongst thousands,[3] in whom my soul is well pleased to dwell all the days of her life.

Verily, thou art my peace-maker, in whom is greatest peace and true rest, out of whom is labor and sorrow and infinite misery.

Verily, thou art a God that hidest thyself,[4] and thy counsel is not with the wicked, but thy speech is with the humble and simple of heart.[5]

Oh, how sweet is thy spirit, O Lord, who to the end thou mightest show forth thy sweetness toward thy children, dost consent to feed them with the bread which is full of all sweetness, even that which cometh down from heaven.[6]

Surely there is no other nation so great,[7] that hath gods so nigh unto them, as thou our God art present to all thy faithful ones, unto whom for their daily comfort, and for the raising up of their hearts to heaven, thou bestowest thyself to be eaten and enjoyed.

3. For what other nation is there of such high renown, as the Christian people?

Or what creature under heaven is there so beloved, as the devout soul, into which God

---

[2]John 15:4   [3]Canticles 5:10   [4]Isaiah 14:15
[5]Prov. 3:34   [6]Wisd. 16:20-21   [7]Deut. 4:7

himself entereth, to nourish it with his glorious flesh?

O unspeakable grace! O admirable condescension! O unmeasurable love specially bestowed on man!

But what return shall I make to the Lord for this grace,[8] for love so unparalleled?

There is nothing else that I am able to present more acceptable, than to offer my heart wholly to my God, and to unite it most inwardly unto him.

Then shall all my inward parts rejoice, when my soul shall be perfectly united unto God.

Then will he say unto me, "If thou art willing to be with me, I am willing to be with thee."

And I will answer him, "Consent, O Lord, to remain with me, for I will gladly be with thee.

"This is my whole desire, that my heart be united unto thee."

CHAPTER 14

Of the Fervent Desire of Some Devout Persons to Receive the Body of Christ

The voice of the disciple.

Oh, how great is the abundance of thy sweetness, O Lord, which thou hast laid up for them that fear thee![1]

---

[8] Psalm 116:12   [1] Psalm 31:19

When I call to mind some devout persons, who approach to thy sacrament, O Lord, with the greatest devotion and affection, I am oftentimes confounded and blush within myself, that I come with such lukewarmness, yea coldness, to thy altar and the table of sacred communion.

I grieve to think that I remain so dry, and without hearty affection to thee; that I am not wholly inflamed in thy presence, O my God, nor so earnestly drawn and affected, as many devout persons have been, who out of a vehement desire of the holy communion, and a feeling affection of heart, could not restrain themselves from tears; but with the mouth of their hearts and bodies alike, they from their inmost souls panted after thee, O God the fountain of life, not being otherwise able to allay or satisfy their hunger, but by receiving thy body with all delight and spiritual eagerness.

2. Oh, the truly ardent faith of those persons! amounting to a probable evidence of thy sacred presence.

For they truly know their Lord in the breaking of bread,[2] whose heart within them so vehemently burneth, whilst thou, O blessed Jesus, dost walk and converse with them.

Such desire and devotion as this, love and fervency so vehement, are often far from me.

Be thou favorable unto me, O merciful Jesus, sweet and gracious Lord, and grant to me thy

[2]Luke 24:32, 35

poor needy creature, sometimes at least in this holy communion to feel if it be but a small portion of thy hearty affectionate love, that my faith may become more strong, my hope in thy goodness may be increased, and that charity once perfectly inflamed, after the tasting of heavenly manna, may never die.

3. But thy mercy is able to grant me the grace which I long for, and in the day when it shall please thee to visit me most mercifully with the spirit of fervor.

For although I burn not with so great desire as those who are so specially devoted to thee, yet notwithstanding, by thy grace I have a desire for this great inflamed desire, praying and longing that I may participate with all such thy fervent lovers, and be numbered among them in their holy company.

CHAPTER 15

That the Grace of Devotion Is Obtained by Humility and Denial of Ourselves

The voice of the Beloved.

Thou oughtest to seek the grace of devotion instantly, to ask it earnestly, to wait for it with patience and confidence, to receive it with gratefulness, humbly to keep it, diligently to work with it, and to commit the term and manner of this heavenly visitation to God, until it shall please him to come unto thee.

Thou oughtest especially to humble thyself, when thou feelest inwardly little or no devotion; and yet not to be too much dejected, nor to grieve inordinately.

God often giveth in one short moment, that which he for a long time denied: he giveth sometimes in the end, that which in the beginning of thy prayer he deferred to grant.

2. If grace should be always presently given, and should be at hand ever with a wish, weak man could not well bear it.

Therefore the grace of devotion is to be waited for with good hope and humble patience.

Nevertheless, do thou impute it to thyself and to thine own sins, when this grace is not given thee, or when it is secretly taken away.

It is sometimes but a small matter that hindereth and hideth grace from us, at least if anything can be called small, and not rather a weighty matter, which obstructeth so great a good.

And if thou remove this, be it great or small, and perfectly overcome it, thou wilt have thy desire.

3. For immediately, as soon as thou givest thyself to God from thy whole heart, and seekest not this nor that, according to thine own pleasure or will, but settlest thyself wholly in him, thou shalt find thyself united and at peace; for nothing will afford so sweet a relish, nothing

be so delightful, as the good pleasure of the divine will.

Whosoever therefore, with a single heart lifts up his intention to God, and keeps himself clear of all inordinate liking or disliking of any created thing, he shall be the most fit to receive grace, and meet for the gift of true devotion.

For the Lord bestoweth his blessings there, where he findeth the vessels empty.

And the more perfectly a person forsaketh these low things, and the more he dieth to himself by contempt of himself, so much the more speedily grace shall come, and shall enter in the more plentifully, and shall lift up the free heart higher and higher.

4. Then shall he see, and flow together, and wonder, and his heart shall be enlarged[1] within him, because the hand of the Lord is with him, and he hath put himself wholly into his hand, even for ever and ever.

Behold, thus shall the man be blessed, who seeketh God with his whole heart, and receiveth not his soul in vain.

This man in receiving the holy eucharist, obtaineth the great favor of divine union; for that he looketh not to his own devotion and comfort, but above all devotion and comfort to the honor and glory of God.

---

[1]Isaiah 55:5

CHAPTER 16

That We Ought to Lay Open Our Necessities to Christ and Crave His Grace

The voice of the disciple.

O Thou most sweet and loving Lord, whom I now desire to receive with all devotion, thou knowest my infirmities, and the necessities which I endure, in how many sins and evils I am involved, how often I am weighed down, tempted, disturbed, and defiled.

Unto thee I come for remedy, I entreat of thee consolation and support.

I speak to thee who knowest all things, to whom all my inward thoughts are open, and who alone canst perfectly comfort and help me

Thou knowest what good things I stand in most need of, and how poor I am in all virtue.

2. Behold, I stand before thee poor and naked, calling for grace, and imploring mercy.

Refresh thy hungry supplicant, inflame my coldness with the fire of thy love, enlighten my blindness with the brightness of thy presence.

Turn thou for me all earthly things into bitterness, all things grievous and contrary into patience, all low and created things into contempt and oblivion.

Lift up my heart to thee in heaven, and do not send me away to wander over the earth.

Be thou only sweet unto me from henceforth

for evermore; for thou alone art my meat and drink, my love and my joy, my sweetness and all my good.

3. Oh, that with thy presence thou wouldest wholly inflame, burn, and conform me unto thyself; that I might be made one spirit with thee,[1] by the grace of inward union, and by the meltings of ardent love!

Suffer me not to go away from thee hungry and dry, but deal mercifully with me, as oftentimes thou hast dealt wonderfully with thy saints.

What marvel is it if I should be wholly inflamed by thee, and fail and come to nothing from myself; since thou art fire always burning and never decaying, love purifying the heart, and enlightening the understanding.

CHAPTER 17

Of Fervent Love, and Vehement Desire to Receive Christ

The voice of the disciple.

With deep devotion and ardent love, with all affection and fervor of heart, I desire to receive thee, O Lord, as many saints and devout persons

---

[1] 1 Cor. 6:17

have desired thee, when they were partakers of thy holy communion; who in holiness of life were to thee most pleasing, and who in devotion also were most fervent.

O my God, everlasting Love, my whole Good, Happiness which can never have an end, I desire to receive thee with the most earnest affection, and the most suitable awe and reverence, that any of the saints ever had, or could feel toward thee.

2. And although I be unworthy to entertain all those feelings of devotion, nevertheless I offer unto thee the whole affection of my heart, as if I were the only one who had all those most pleasing, most ardent longings after thee.

Yea, and all that a dutiful mind can conceive and desire, I do, with the deepest reverence and most inward affection, offer and present unto thee.

I desire to reserve nothing to myself, but freely and most cheerfully to sacrifice unto thee myself and all that is mine.

O Lord, my God, my Creator, and my Redeemer, I do desire to receive thee this day, with such affection, reverence, praise, and honor, with such gratitude, worthiness, and love, with such faith, hope, and purity, as thy most holy mother, the glorious Virgin Mary, received and desired thee, when to the angel who declared unto her glad tidings of the mystery of the incarnation, she humbly and devoutly answered, "Behold the handmaid of the Lord, let it be done unto me according to thy word."[1]

3. And as thy blessed forerunner, the most excellent among the saints, John Baptist, rejoicing in thy presence, leaped for joy of the Holy Ghost, while he was yet shut up in his mother's womb;[2] and afterward, seeing Jesus walking among men, humbled himself very greatly, and said with devout affection, "The friend of the bridegroom that standeth and heareth him, rejoiceth greatly because of the voice of the bridegroom;"[3] in like manner I also wish to be inflamed with great and holy desires, and to offer myself up to thee from my whole heart.

Wherefore also I offer and present unto thee the triumphant joys, the ardent affections, the mental ecstasies, the supernatural illuminations and celestial visions of all devout hearts, with all the virtues and praises celebrated and to be celebrated by all creatures in heaven, and in earth, for myself, and for all such as are commended to me in prayer; that by all thou mayest worthily be praised, and for ever glorified.

4. Receive, O Lord my God, my wishes and desires of giving thee infinite praise, and blessing that hath no bounds, which, according to the measure of thine ineffable greatness, are most justly due unto thee.

These praises I render unto thee, and desire to render every day and every moment. And with

---

[1]Luke 1:38   [2]Luke 1:44   [3]John 3:29

all entreaty and affectionateness I do invite and beseech all heavenly spirits, and all thy faithful servants, to render with me thanks and praises unto thee.

5. Let all people, nations, and languages, praise thee,[4] and magnify thy holy and most delicious name, with highest exultation and ardent devotion.

And let all who reverently and devoutly celebrate thy most high sacrament, and receive it with full faith, be accounted worthy to find grace and mercy at thy hands, and pray with humble supplication in behalf of me a sinner.

And when they shall have attained to their desired devotion, and joyful union with thee, and shall have departed from thy holy heavenly table, well comforted and marvellously refreshed, Oh, let them agree to remember my poor soul.

CHAPTER 18

That a Man Should Not Be a Curious Searcher Into the Holy Sacrament, But an Humble Follower of Christ, Submitting His Sense to Divine Faith

The voice of the Beloved.

Thou must beware of curious and unprofitable searching into this most profound sacrament, if

---

[4] Psalm 117

thou wilt not be plunged into the depths of doubt.

"He that is a searcher of my Majesty, shall be overpowered by the glory of it:[1] God is able to work more than man can understand.

A dutiful and humble inquiry after the truth is allowable, provided we be always ready to be taught, and study to walk according to the sound opinions of the Fathers.

2. It is a blessed simplicity when a man leaves the difficult ways of questions and disputings, and goes on forward in the plain and firm path of God's commandments.

Many have lost devotion while they sought to search into things too high.

Faith is required at thy hands, and a sincere life, not height of understanding, nor deep inquiry into the mysteries of God.

If thou dost not understand, nor conceive these things that are under thee, how shalt thou be able to comprehend those that are above thee?

Submit thyself unto God, and humble thy sense to faith, and the light of knowledge shall be given thee, in such degree as shall be profitable and necessary for thee.

3. Some are grievously tempted about faith and the holy sacrament, this is not to be imputed to themselves, but rather to the enemy.

Be not thou anxious; do not dispute with

[1]Prov. 25:27

thine own thoughts, nor give any answer to doubts suggested by the devil; but trust the words of God, trust his saints and prophets, and the wicked enemy will flee from thee.

It oftentimes is very profitable to the servant of God to endure such things.

For the devil tempts not unbelievers and sinners, whom he has already secure possession of, but faithful and religious devout persons he in various ways tempts and vexes.

4. Go forward therefore with simple and undoubting faith, and with the reverence of a supplicant approach thou this holy sacrament; and whatsoever thou art not able to understand, commit securely to Almighty God.

God deceiveth thee not; he is deceived that trusteth too much to himself.

God walketh with the simple,[2] revealeth himself to the humble, giveth understanding to the little ones, openeth the sense to pure minds, and hideth grace from the curious and proud.

Human reason is feeble and may be deceived, but true faith can not be deceived.

5. All reason and natural search ought to follow faith, not to go before it, nor to break in upon it.

For faith and love do here specially take the lead, and work in hidden ways, in this most holy, most supremely excellent sacrament.

God, who is eternal and incomprehensible,

---

[2]Psalm 19:7; 119:130; Matt. 11:29

and of infinite power, doeth things great and unsearchable in heaven and in earth, and there is no tracing out of his marvellous works.

If the works of God were such, as that they might be easily comprehended by human reason, they could not be justly called marvellous or unspeakable.

INDEX

Numbers after each entry indicate Book Number and chapter in which the entry is found.

[329]

of the imitation of his life, *1. 1,* p. 23;
3. 56, p. 260:

happiness of him who has Christ for his
teacher, *1. 3,* p. 27:

we should obey our superiors after his
example, *3. 13,* p. 156.

See Jesus.

Comfort. *See* Consolation.

Communion. *See* Holy communion.

Complaint, we ought not lightly to complain,
2. 1, p. 91.

Compunction, benefit of, *1. 1,* p. 24:
commendation of it, *1. 21,* p. 65:
compunction of heart, whence it arises,
    id. p. 67:

how it is to be obtained, *1. 20,* p. 60.

Concupiscence, the pleasures thereof brief and
false, *3. 12,* pp. 154-55:

must be contended with, *3. 35,* pp. 206-7:
may not be yielded to, *3. 12,* p. 155.

Confession, of infirmity and misery,
    1. 21, p. 67; *22,* p. 69.

Confidence, of recovering grace, *3. 30,* p. 194:
our confidence to be reposed in God under
    injuries, *3. 46,* pp. 227-28:

not in one's self or in others, *1. 7,*
pp. 34-35; *20,* pp. 60-61.

Conquer, to subdue one's self should be our
daily study, *1. 3,* p. 29.

See Mortification.

Conscience, the comfort of a good conscience,
    1. 20, p. 61; *2. 6,* pp. 100-102:
a bad conscience has no peace, *id.* ibid.

have to God, *4. 7*, p. 296; *8*, p. 297;
9, p. 299.

See Eucharist.

Holy Spirit, the renewing of the Spirit is like
the cleansing of iron from rust by the force
of fire, *2. 4*, p. 97.

See Amendment of life.

Holy Trinity, disputes concerning the, not
edifying unless conducted with humility,
1. 1, p. 24.

Home, better that a man should remain at
home, *1. 20*, p. 61.

Honor, to be despised,
3. 41, p. 218.

Hope, our hope and confidence should be
placed in God alone,
1. 7, p. 35; *3. 59*, p. 270:
he that hopes in God's help should meanwhile do what lies in his own power,
1. 25, p. 83.

Humility, obtained in communion
4. 15, p. 320:
the humble man accounts himself vile,
3. 8, p. 145:
all the saints were humble, *2. 10*, p. 113:
how God deals with the humble,
2. 2, p. 93:
the humble enjoy much peace, *2. 6*, p. 101:
we should humble ourselves beneath all
men, *1. 7*, p. 36:
duty of humble self-submission,
2. 2, p. 93:

he the most fit to receive them who
    accounts himself unworthy of them,
      id., p. 178.

Lukewarmness in religion a bad sign,
    1. 11, p. 40.

Man is a liar, therefore not easily to be trusted,
    3. 45, p. 225:
    in this world is as a stranger and an exile,
      1. 23, p. 76:
    a spiritually-minded man never wholly lets
      himself loose to things external,
      2. 1, p. 88:
    a man should count himself unworthy of all
      consolation, *3. 52*, p. 246:
    evils befalling him who does not carefully
      look to himself, *2. 5*, p. 98.

Master, happy is he who has Christ for his
    master and instructer, *1. 3*, p. 27.

Mercies of God. *See* Loving-kindnesses.

Merits, our spiritual state not to be estimated by
    the consolations we experience,
    3. 7, p. 141.

Mind, the mind lays open its wants to God, that
    so it may be freed from the dangers of sin,
    3. 26, p. 187:
    prayer for mental illumination,
      3. 23, p. 182.

Miracles, it is better than the power of working
    miracles to be able to be quiet and do one's
    duty, *1. 20*, p. 63.

Misery, human misery is great, *1. 22*, p. 68;
    3. 20, p. 172:

Silence, benefit of, *1. 20*, p. 63.

Simple, the pure and simple-hearted are taught of God, *1. 3*, p. 28:
> there should be simplicity in our intentions, and purity in our affections, *2. 4*, p. 96.

Sincerity. *See* Walking.

Sins are the fuel of infernal fire, *1. 24*, p. 78:
> of the punishment laid up for sinners, *id.*, ibid.:
> no sin ever to be committed for any cause whatever, *1. 15*, p. 48:
> human nature is prone to sin, *1. 22*, p. 69.

Slanderers, their tongues to be disregarded, *3. 28*, p. 191.

Slothfulness, evil of spiritual, *1. 25*, p. 84.

Solitude, sometimes to be sought, *1. 20*, p. 60.

Sorrow. *See* Grief.

Spirit. *See* Holy Spirit.

Spiritual things, impeded by the necessities of the body, *1. 22*, p. 69.

Strangers. *See* Foreigners.

Study, our constant study should be to master ourselves, *1. 3*, p. 29:
> also to root out what is wrong, and to plant what is right, *id.*, p. 30.

Subjection. *See* Submission.

Submission, a submissive temper most valuable, *1. 9*, p. 37.

Suffering, he who has learnt to suffer perceives God's aid granted to him, *2. 2*, p. 93:
> he who can not suffer a little now, how will

the whole life of man is trial, *id.*, p. 43;
3. *35*, p. 206:

rewards promised to those who endure
trials aright, 3. *49*, p. 239:

for some men it is better not to be
altogether free from them, *1. 20*, p. 62:

no security against them in this life,
3. *35*, p. 206:

nor any end to them here, *id.*, ibid.
See Patience.

Tribulation, necessary for man, *1. 13*, p. 44:

its great benefit, *1. 12*, p. 42:

we should glory in it, *2. 6*, p. 100:

it makes us feel our dependence on God,
1. 12, p. 43:

he shall find nothing but tribulation who
seeks anything else but God only,
1. 17, p. 52:

all the saints suffered tribulations,
1. 13, p. 44.

See Trials.

Trinity. *See* Holy.

Troubles, not to mix ourselves up with other
men's, *1. 11*, p. 40.

Trust, we may not trust all men, 3. *45*, p. 224:

men more easily believe ill than good of
others, *1. 4*, p. 31:

all our trust must be set on God,
1. 7, p. 34; *2. 1*, p. 89; *3. 59*, p. 270:

we must be careful of placing too much
confidence in ourselves, *2. 5*, p. 98:

Truth, to be loved above all things, *3. 4*, p. 133:

wherein true wisdom consists, *1. 1*, p. 24:

a point of wisdom not to be hasty in action, nor to trust too much to what we hear, *1. 4*, p. 31:

he is wise who estimates things as they are, *2. 1*, p. 91:

those who are wise in their own conceits are in danger, *3. 7*, p. 144.

See Self-estimation.

Women, familiarity with them to be avoided by those who have devoted themselves to a monastic life, *1. 8*, p. 36.

Word, Christ's words to the faithful soul, *3. 1*, p. 125:

to slip in word is but too easy, *3. 45*, p. 224:

superfluous words to be cut away, *1. 10*, p. 38:

reproachful words to be borne patiently, *3. 46*, p. 227:

to be disregarded, *id.*, ibid.:

benefit of religious conversation, *1. 10*, p. 39.

Works and exercises, religious, should be done as in God's presence, *1. 19*, p. 56:

a good work sometimes may properly be intermitted, *1. 15*, p. 48; *19*, p. 57:

any work done in charity is fruitful, *1. 15*, p. 48:

humble works to be persisted in when we can not attend to higher, *3. 51*, p. 245:

in some works the motive is supposed to be
  charity when it is mere sensuality,
    1. 15, p. 49:
he works much, who loves much,
    id., ibid.:
our works to be inwardly arranged before
  they come abroad, *1. 19*, p. 58:
works not done in charity are useless,
    1. 15, p. 49.
World, a privilege to be enabled to despise it,
  and to follow Christ, *3. 10*, p. 149.
Wordly men, have their crosses, *3. 12*, p. 154.
Years. *See* Conversion.
Zeal, passion is sometimes mistaken for it,
  2. 5, p. 98:
  should rather be directed against ourselves
  than others, *2. 3*, p. 95.